Guido Pe[...]

TUSCAN
CUISINE

BOOK OF RECIPES

G GIUNTI DᴇMᴇᴛRᴀ

Texts and illustrations are partially taken from:
Guido Pedrittoni, *Cucina toscana*
Demetra 1999

Editing and layout
Paola Agostini e Mariarosa Brizzi

Graphic design
Matteo Lucii

Photographs
Giunti Archives

Translation
Lexis, Florence – Revised by Catherine Frost

www.giunti.it

© 2007 Giunti Editore S.p.A.
Via Bolognese 165 - 50139 Firenze - Italia
Via Dante 4 - 20121 Milano - Italia
New edition: March 2007

Reprint							Year			
6	5	4	3	2	1	0	2010	2009	2008	2007

Printed by Giunti Industrie Grafiche S.p.A. – Prato (Italy)

Introduction

Tuscan cuisine has developed in one of the most fertile regions in Italy, where the abundance of olive groves, vines, pasture for livestock, fields for corn and vegetables and a sea full of fish, have given birth to a tradition whose simplicity is never a synonym of poverty. With its honest, genuine and robust flavours, it is a perfect reflection of the straightforward character of its creators.

Its basic ingredients recur with amazing frequency: beans, peas, chick peas, broad beans, game, ox, fowl and pig offal, artichokes, cardoons, chestnuts, celery, onions and garlic – absent only in sweet dishes- and rosemary, present even in these!

From this array of simple ingredients the traditional dishes, with their roots firmly embedded in time-honoured peasant culture, come to life. "Ribollita", a sublime way to make use of leftovers from bean soup. "Panzanella", once a peasant snack and now a sophisticated starter in a rustic style menu. Then there's "cibreo", made with offal, and "scottiglia", an excellent mixed stew. Even the sweets are simple and substantial, unencumbered by lush creams: from "cantuccini di Prato" to "ricciarelli" and "panforte di Siena", their goodness lies in the quality of their ingredients and their tasteful blending without frills which could spoil the wholesome flavor. The only adornment necessary, indeed, almost indispensable, to accompany these sweets is a glass of irresistible "vinsanto", the logical conclusion to a Tuscan dinner worth its name.

What else is there? Olive oil, the supreme seasoning whether used for cooking or added as a dressing to the finished product. Then there are the cheeses, many of them made from sheep's milk. There are the vegetables and pulses with which to prepare tasty side dishes that are substantial enough to qualify as main dishes in their own right.

To complete the picture we need a glass of good wine chosen from among Chianti or Brunello or Nobile di Montepulciano, Bianco di Pitigliano or Vernaccia di San Gimignano, to mention just a few of the many excellent wines that grace the tables of the region.

Conversion chart

WEIGHT AND LENGTH	CORRESPONDES TO	
1 gram (g)	0.035 ounces	(divide by 28 to find ounces)
1 hectogram (hg)	3.57 ounces	(divide by 0.28 to find ounces)
1 kilogram (kg)	2.2 pounds	(divide by 0.45 to find pounds)
1 millilitre (ml)	0.03 fluid ounces	(divide by 30 to find fluid ounces)
1 litre (litro)	2.1 pints	(multiply by 2.1 to find pints)
	3.8 gallons (U.S.)	(divide by 0.26 to find U.S. gallons)
	0.22 gallons (U.K.)	(divide by 4.5 to find U.K. gallons)
1 centimeter (cm)	0.4 inches	(multiply by 0.4 to find inches)
1 millimeter (mm)	0.04 inches	(multiply by 0.04 to find inches)
1 meter (m)	3.3 feet	(multiply by 3.3 to find feet)

TEMPERATURE		
Celsius degree (°C)	(°C x 1.8) + 32 to find Farenheit degree (°F)	
	180 °C correspondes to 356 °F	
Farenheit degree (°F)	(°F - 32) x 555 to find Celsius degree (°C)	
	392 °F correspondes to 200 °C	

Note for the reader
- *Unless otherwise indicated, the recipes are for 4 person.*
- *The salt, pepper and water used in the recipes are not listed among the ingredients – except in special cases – since it is taken for granted that always present in the kitchen.*
- *Extra-virgin olive oil is abbreviated as e.v. olive oil.*
- *The basic preparations (such as fresh pasta dough or meat sauce), when utilised in several recipes, are described in the yellow inserts to which readers are referred.*
- *Other inserts contain additional information on particular recipes, ingredients or traditions.*

Starters

Cecina
(Chick pea pancake)

Chick pea pancake is a typical, easy to prepare snack which lends itself as an unusual but tasty starter. Dilute the chick pea flour in the water. Leave it to settle, then stir with a wooden spoon. Add the oil and a pinch of salt. Pour the mixture into a wide, low-sided baking tin. Bear in mind that the chick pea pancake must not be thicker than 1/2 cm, so if you haven't got a wide enough tin, it is better to cook two lots. Put the tin in a preheated oven and bake until a golden crust has formed. Serve generously sprinkled with freshly ground black pepper.

Ingredients
500 g of chick pea flour
2 l of water
1 glass of e.v. olive oil
whole black pepper

Recommended wine
Montescudaio bianco

Crostini bianconeri
(Black-n-white toast)

Melt half the butter in a terrine over gentle heat. Then add some of the grated parmesan and the finely chopped onion. In a small saucepan, blend the meat extract with the remaining soft butter to form a light cream.

At this point lightly toast the slices of bread in the oven. Brush them with the melted butter and parme-

Ingredients
50 g butter
30 g parmesan
20 g black truffle
1/2 tablespoon of chopped onion
10 g meat extract
8 slices of country-style bread

Recommended wine
Parrina bianco

san. Leave to cool, then spread with the creamy mixture. Grate the cleaned truffle on top and arrange the slices on a serving dish according to taste.

Crostini di fegatini - 1
(Chicken liver croûtons - 1)

Ingredients

350 g chicken liver
1 small onion
100 g butter
1/2 cup meat stock
1/2 glass vinsanto (scant)
2 egg yolks
1/4 cup soft bread
50 g pickled capers
and gherkins
16 slices of country-style
(or sandwich bread)

Melt the butter in a saucepan and gently sauté the finely sliced onion until soft. Add the finely chopped chicken liver. Sauté for a few minutes stirring continuously with a wooden spoon. Then add the wine.

In the meantime, blend the egg yolks with a bit of broth and pour them into the saucepan. Stir with a wooden spoon and cook for about 20 minutes. Chop the pickled capers and gherkins and blend with the soft bread which has previously been soaked in vinegar, squeezed dry and crumbled. Add this mixture to the pan and stir vigorously. Add a pinch of salt and pepper, remove from the heat and set aside to rest. Lightly brush the toasted bread with melted butter and then spread with the mixture. Arrange on a dish and garnish.

Recommended wine
*Bianco Pisano
di San Torpè*

Crostini di fegatini - 2
(Chicken liver croûtons - 2)

Ingredienti

250 g chicken liver
50 g bacon
2 fresh spring onions
1 carrot, 1 stalk of celery
30 g butter
20 g dried mushrooms
1/2 lemon, parsley
1 cup of stock
1 baguette

First clean the spring onions, the celery and the carrot. Then finely chop the vegetables and bacon, and sauté in butter in an earthenware pot. Meanwhile wash the mushrooms and leave to soak in warm water. Clean and wash the chicken livers. When the vegetables are soft, add the mushrooms, liver, salt and pepper. Leave to absorb the flavours for about 15 minutes and then add the hot stock.

Simmer, stirring frequently with a wooden spoon, for another 15 minutes.

Slice the baguette into rounds.

When the liver is done, remove it and the mushrooms from the stock and chop finely.

Put them back in the pot with the parsley and a little lemon juice. Spread the mixture on the bread slices and serve.

Recommended wine
Bianco di Pitigliano

TUSCAN BREAD

Ingredients
1.4 kg of bread flour
60 g of baker's yeast
water

To make Tuscan bread, notoriously salt-free, knead the flour with the yeast and enough water to obtain the right consistency. Knead the dough very well, then cover it with a dry cloth and leave it to rest for about 6 hours.

Then knead the dough again, divide it into 5 parts and shape them in the form of loaves. Lightly score the top of each loaf with a knife, bake in a moderate oven (220 °C) for about 40 minutes until the crust is golden and crunchy.

The bread is done when the inside is dry and fluffy and the crust is crunchy. This is the perfect bread to be sliced and used for "bruschette", "crostoni" and" fettunta".

Crostini di milza (Spleen on toast)

Ingredients

250 g of calf's spleen
2 anchovies preserved in salt
2 tablespoons of salted capers
1/4 glass of dry white wine
1 tablespoon of stock
butter
e.v. olive oil
8 slices of stale bread

Peel and slice the onion. Remove the skin from the spleen, then clean, wash, dry and cut into pieces. Next, sauté the spleen in oil and butter with the onion for about 5 minutes, preferably in an earthenware pot, stirring continuously with a wooden spoon. Remove from the heat and leave to cool a little. Remove the spleen and the onion from the pot and chop very finely with an ordinary knife or better still a mincing knife.

Put the chopped spleen and onion back in the pot and return to the heat. Add a little more butter and oil and stir with a wooden spoon to obtain a smooth cream. Dilute with the white wine, stirring continuously until it evaporates. If necessary, add a little stock. Cover the pot and simmer about 45 minutes.

In the meantime wash the anchovies, removing salt and bones. Chop them together with the capers, which have been rinsed in cold water. Stir carefully into the spleen mixture which has been removed from the heat. Lastly, toast the slices of bread. Sprinkle them with a little stock and spread with the mixture.

Recommended wine
*Bianco Pisano
di San Torpè*

Crostini maremmani (Maremma croûtons)

Ingredients

300 g chicken liver
50 g minced pork
1/2 glass of vinsanto
1 onion, 3 cloves of garlic
1 carrot, 1 stalk of celery
3 sage leaves
1 sprig of fresh rosemary
e.v. olive oil
1 baguette

Peel the onion and garlic and clean the carrot and celery. Chop the vegetables and sauté them in an earthenware pot with a bit of oil, the sage and rosemary. Wash and chop the chicken liver. Add to the vegetables together with the minced pork and stir them to absorb the flavours. Add the wine and cook with the lid

on for 45 minutes. Meanwhile cut the baguette into rounds. Lastly, roughly chop the cooked meat, then put it back on the heat for a few moments. Now it is ready to be spread on the oven-grilled bread.

Serve the "crostini" steaming hot.

Recommended wine
Bianco Pisano
di San Torpè

Crostoni ai funghi
(Mushroom croûtons)

Ingredients
650 g cep mushrooms
1 clove of garlic
1 small onion
a handful of fresh parsley
1 tablespoon of salted capers
1 cup of stock
1 tablespoon of butter
1 tablespoon e.v. olive oil
16 slices of country-style bread

Clean the mushrooms and rinse them quickly under running water. Dry them with a clean towel. Clean, wash and dry the parsley. Then chop the mushrooms with the garlic, the onion and some of the parsley.

Heat the oil and butter in a pan. Add the chopped ingredients. Cook over a medium heat, adding a bit of stock if necessary. Meanwhile, rinse the capers under running water and then chop them with the remaining

Tuscan extra-virgin olive oil

Olive oil is one of the basic ingredients of Tuscan cooking. It has given rise, in fact, to a sort of "cult" of top quality oil, probably originating from the typical apportionment of olive oil production and the olive-pressing process (often in family-run olive mills), characteristic of the region.

Hearty and subtle at the same time, undoubtedly one of the world's finest, Tuscan extra-virgin olive oil is an ingredient of sauces of every kind, of meat and seafood dishes, and is used with vegetables both cooked and raw. The oil produced around Lucca, deriving from the Frantoio and Leccino varieties, is generally lighter and more fruity in flavour; oil from the Province of Grosseto tends to be stronger, with a taste that is savoury and distinctive; the oils from the hills Florentine Hills are fine and delicate, while those from the Chianti area have a stronger taste, which is even more pronounced in the Province of Arezzo.

parsley. Just before removing from the heat, taste for salt and pepper and add the chopped capers and parsley. Lastly, gently fry the slices of bread in a frying pan with a tablespoon of butter, or simply toast them in the oven. Cover them with plenty of the mushroom spread, arrange on a serving dish and garnish with sprigs of parsley.

Recommended wine
Vermentino bianco

Striscioline (Striplets)

Ingredients
200 g of calf's head (or pig's)
2 medium-sized onions
2 lettuce hearts
1 green tomato
1 medium-sized pepper
40 g of stoned black olives
wine vinegar
e.v. olive oil

This unusual salad can be prepared using either a calf or a pig's head. Once the head has been boiled, cut it up into thin strips. Place these in a glass or earthenware dish. Sprinkle with vinegar and then leave in a cool place to rest for a while. Meanwhile, finely chop the onions. Wash, dry and prepare the tomato, pepper and the lettuce hearts, cutting everything into little strips. Discard the tomato seeds. Add to the calf's head and season with salt, pepper, oil and a bit more vinegar. Mix everything together carefully. Lastly, add the black olives and serve.

Recommended wine
Bianco di Pitigliano

Totani in insalata
(Squid salad)

Ingredients
500 g fresh squid
1 bunch radishes, 2 carrots
3 stalks white celery
1 stalk green celery
1/2 fennel, 1/2 onion
1 leek
1 bay leaf
e.v. olive oil
whole black pepper

Wash the squid and boil in lightly salted water with the green celery, the onion and the bay leaf. When they are cooked, drain and cut into strips. Put these strips into a large terrine. Clean and wash the remaining vegetables. Slice the white celery, the fennel, the car-

rots and the white part of the leek but leave the radishes whole. Stir the vegetables and the squid together gently. Season with salt and freshly ground pepper and plenty of e.v. olive oil.

Recommended wine
Bianco di Pitigliano

Fettunta (Toast with oil and garlic) ▶▶

Ingredients

4 slices of country-style bread (preferably at least one day old)
2 cloves of garlic
whole black pepper
e.v. olive oil

"Fettunta" is wonderfully simple to prepare, its success depending largely on the quality of the oil; ideally, it should come from cold-pressed olives. Toast the bread lightly over a barbecue (or under the oven grill).

As soon as the surface is crisp, rub the slices with garlic. Sprinkle with a pinch of salt and freshly ground black pepper. Then pour olive oil onto each slice and serve immediately while still very hot and before the oil soaks into the bread completely.

Recommended wine
Montescudaio rosso

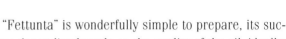

Lard from Colonnata

For centuries, the lard prepared in Colonnata, a little town in the Province of Carrara, has been aged in tubs carved out of a rare kind of marble that is resistant even to the corrosion of a strong brine. These tubs are placed in cellars excavated in the rock, where the natural moisture and the porosity of the walls provide the ideal natural conditions for ageing the lard. The ageing procedure is the following: the inside of each tub is rubbed all over with garlic, then the bottom is covered with a layer of sea salt, aromatic herbs and spices, on which the strips of lard are laid. Then comes another layer of salt, aromatic herbs and spices, and then strips of lard again, until the tub is full. The tubs have different sizes, and some are even large enough to hold several quintals. After a week, the tubs are reopened and a mixture of water and salt is poured into them, forming a thick brine.

From this moment on, except for a few rare inspections to check the state of the brine, nothing else need by done until the conclusion of the process, 6-10 months later.

Sauces

Ragù della domenica
(Sunday meat sauce)

Ingredients
200 g lean tender beef
100 g lean pork
1 sausage
1 small onion
1 carrot
1 stalk of celery
1 glass of red wine
200 g peeled tomatoes
1 cup of stock
whole pepper
e.v. olive oil

Peel and chop the onion, celery and carrot. Soften the vegetables over a moderate heat in a little oil, preferably in an earthenware pot. Meanwhile chop the meat into small pieces and break up the sausage. Add all this to the sautéed vegetables, and leave to stew gently. Add a little warm stock, let it reduce slightly, then sprinkle with the red wine. When this has evaporated, add the chopped tomatoes and a little more stock. Season with salt and simmer for about an hour on a low heat. When it is done, season with a little freshly ground pepper.

Salsa di magro per lesso
(Green sauce for boiled meat)

Ingredients
1 cup mixed pickles
1 tablespoon of salted capers
1 clove of garlic
a handful of fresh parsley
1 sprig of tarragon
1 hard-boiled egg
mayonnaise

On a large wooden cutting board, place the peeled garlic, rinsed capers, drained pickles, parsley and tarragon; mince with a big knife or a mincing knife until the ingredients are sufficiently finely chopped. Pour into a terrine and add the hard-boiled egg which has been put through a sieve and a little olive oil. Mix carefully to blend the ingredients. Then add the mayonnaise, still stirring slowly and carefully to obtain a satisfactory consistency. To be served chilled.

Salsa rossa piccante (Hot red sauce)

Ingredients
2 big sweet red peppers
1 clove of garlic
1/4 cup soft bread
1/2 glass of vinegar
paprika
e.v. olive oil

Place the soft bread in a bowl with the vinegar and leave to soak. Meanwhile, roast the peppers in the oven or over a burner on top of the stove. Then leave to cool, skin and remove seeds. Squeeze the bread to remove the excess moisture and stir in into the chopped peppers and garlic. Place in a bowl. Stir in a pinch of paprika and enough olive oil to form a creamy mixture.

Salsa verde (Green sauce)

Ingredients
1 clove of garlic
2 teaspoons of salted capers
2 gherkins
2 anchovy fillets preserved in oil
1 small onion
1 sprig of tarragon
1 hard-boiled egg
a fistful of soft bread
a bunch of fresh parsley
wine vinegar
e.v. olive oil
hot red pepper (optional)

Put the vinegar in a bowl. Add the bread, leave it to soften, then squeeze and chop it with the mincing knife together with the parsley, tarragon, the capers rinsed in running water, and the hard-boiled egg. Put all this into a suitable bowl and mix, adding enough olive oil to obtain the right consistency. Sprinkle with a few drops of vinegar. Season with salt and pepper and, if you like it hot, with a little chopped hot red pepper. Then cover the sauce and leave to rest in a cool place for a few hours.

Salsa verde semplice
(Simple green sauce)

Ingredients
2 cloves of garlic
a bunch of fresh parsley
e.v. olive oil

This recipe, a simplification of the one for classic green sauce, is really quick and easy to prepare.

Chop the garlic and parsley. Place a bowl and add salt, pepper and oil, stirring until you obtain the right consistency. This sauce, in addition to accompanying meat and hard-boiled eggs, can also be used as an emergency sauce for pasta or rice, or to flavour stocks and soups.

 # Soups

Acquacotta (Vegetable soup) - 1

Ingredients

500 g cep mushrooms
250 g tomatoes
1 clove garlic
1 l of water
3 eggs
50 g grated parmesan
8 slices stale bread
1/4 cup e.v. olive oil

Clean the mushrooms very gently. With a small knife scrape the stalks. Wash and dry and then cut them into thin strips. Heat the oil in a casserole and add the peeled garlic. When it starts to turn golden, add the mushrooms and season lightly with salt and pepper. Continue to cook over a gentle heat stirring occasionally with a wooden spoon. Meanwhile, peel and chop the tomatoes (after briefly plunging them in boiling water to loosen the peel). Add them to the mushrooms. Add 1 litre of boiling salted water and continue cooking. Toast the bread slices, then place them in individual soup bowls. Break the eggs into a soup tureen, add some of the grated parmesan and beat with a spoon. Then add the mushroom soup. Pour the soup into the bowls on top of the toasted bread and sprinkle with grated parmesan.

Recommended wine
Chianti Colline Pisane

An ancient soup

"Acquacotta" is a thick soup, typical of the Maremma area stretching over part of Tuscany and Lazio, and of the poorer hilly parts of Umbria. The basic ingredients of the original recipe can be traced merely by looking at one of the poorest and perhaps most ancient versions: wild herbs, onion, garlic, whole wheat bread, aromatic herbs, olive oil or lard, wine, salt, pepper or hot red pepper. As can be seen, tomatoes were not used, and the acidulous flavour so distinctive of this soup was conferred by verjuice, the fermented juice of unripe grapes.

Other versions of this recipe contain ingredients such as bacon and even stockfish. And some of them add potatoes, carrots and pecorino as well.

 **SOUPS**

Acquacotta (Vegetable soup) - 2

Ingredients
400 g puréed tomatoes
350 g sweet peppers
4 eggs
2 onions
2 stalks of celery
1 l of water
100 g Tuscan bread
grated parmesan
whole pepper
2.5 dl of e.v. olive oil

Peel and finely chop the onions. Soften them in an earthenware casserole in a little oil. Then add the peppers and celery which have previously been washed and cut in pieces, discarding the seeds and interior filaments of the peppers. Sauté for about 10 minutes over low heat, then add the puréed tomatoes. Season with salt and pepper and let the sauce evaporate for about 20 minutes before adding 1 litre of boiling lightly salted water. Bring to the boil again and simmer for about 15 minutes. Meanwhile, pour the beaten eggs into a soup tureen and season with freshly ground black pepper. Now pour the boiling soup into the tureen, stirring gently, and sprinkle with grated parmesan. In each soup bowl, place a slice of bread that has been toasted in the oven; ladle the hot soup over it.

Recommended wine
Parrina rosso

Cipollata (Onion soup)

Ingredients
600 g white onions
100 g sausage
50 g cured ham
1 l of water
4 slices country-style bread
2 tablespoons grated parmesan
e.v. olive oil

Peel the onions and blanch them for a few minutes in boiling water. Then drain and leave to cool. Break up the sausage, chop the cured ham and sauté the mixture gently in a little oil, preferably in an earthenware pot. When the mixture is golden, add the finely sliced onions and sauté gently over very low heat. Add 1 litre of water and boil for a good 30 minutes so that any scum rising to the surface can be removed. Taste for salt. At this point, toast the slices of country-style bread in the oven. Place them in individual bowls. Sprinkle with grated parmesan and ladle out the soup.

Recommended wine
Chianti Rufina

Garmugia
(Rich vegetable soup)

Ingredients
150 g lean minced beef
80 g bacon
6 artichokes
1 bunch of asparagus
100 g fresh broad beans
100 g fresh peas
100 g beet leaves
2 onions
1 stalk of celery
1 carrot
1 lemon
1 l of stock
e.v. olive oil
toasted rounds of bread

x 5. = 2viperfer

Clean and wash the vegetables. Cut the artichokes into quarters and soak for about 1/2 hour in water and lemon juice. Boil the asparagus in salted water.

When it is half cooked, drain and put the tips aside. Boil the beet leaves, press the water out of them and chop.

Sauté the finely sliced onion, celery and carrot in a little oil until tender.

Then add the minced beef and the coarsely chopped bacon, stirring it gently to let it absorb the flavours for at least 10 minutes.

When the meat has browned, add all the vegetables. Season with salt and pepper and sprinkle with a ladleful of warm stock.

After about 1/2 an hour add the rest of the stock and continue to cook for about 90 minutes.

Serve the soup with toasted rounds of bread.

Recommended wine
Bianco di Pitigliano

Broth for festive occasions

According to a famous proverb, "an old hen makes good broth" and this recipe is the proof of that ancient popular wisdom. Let's see, then, how to prepare really good meat broth.

Fill a large pot with about 5 l of water, add 1 kg of lean beef, 1 old hen, 2 onions, 2 carrots, 2 stalks of celery and 2-3 ripe tomatoes. Bring to a boil and simmer for about 2 hours, until the liquid has reduced to about half. Add the salt and pour it through a fine-mesh sieve. Cut the chicken and veal into small pieces and serve the broth and the meat separately.

For Christmas, stuffed capon may be used instead of a hen.

The broth in which it has cooked, mixed with ordinary broth, is ideal for cooking the "tortelli".

Gran farro
(Spelt soup)

Ingredients
200 g dried red beans
100 g spelt
100 g peeled tomatoes
1 onion
1 carrot
1 stalk of celery
1 clove of garlic
4 basil leaves
1 sage leaf
marjoram
nutmeg
1 ladleful of broth
e.v. olive oil
whole black pepper

Start the evening before by soaking the beans and removing the impurities from the spelt. Wash it in water so that the husks come to the surface. The next day, drain the beans, then cook them in a large pot of water. Put the cooking-water aside and then blend the beans to a smooth cream. Boil the spelt separately for about 3 hours.

Clean and chop the onion, carrot, celery, garlic, sage and marjoram and then sauté them in a little oil in a large pan.

When the vegetables start to turn golden, add the chopped tomatoes, spices, salt and pepper. Simmer for a few minutes before adding the beans and the spelt and their cooking-water. Cook for about 20 minutes stirring carefully. Add a little warm stock if the soup is too thick.

A few minutes before removing from the heat, add the chopped basil. Serve the soup, adding some e.v. olive oil and a pinch of freshly ground black pepper.

Recommended wine
Montescudaio rosso

Infarinata
(Cabbage and bean soup with cornmeal)

Ingredients
450 g cornmeal
400 g fresh red beans
300 g winter cabbage
2 pork rinds
1 onion, 1 carrot
2 cloves of garlic
1 stalk of celery
rosemary, basil
wild fennel seeds
e.v. olive oil

Shell the beans and boil them in salted water together with the rinds.

Meanwhile, clean and slice the onion, celery and carrot and sauté in a large pan with the crushed garlic and a little oil.

When the onion starts to soften add the cleaned, washed and chopped winter cabbage. Stir and leave to soak up the flavours for a few minutes before adding the beans, 3/4 cooked, and their cooking-water.

Taste for salt and cover. Simmer for about 1/2 an hour. At this point sprinkle the surface of the soup with the maize flour.

Stir and cook for another 3/4 hour, stirring frequently so the flour does not form lumps.

Serve the infarinata hot or cold. When cold, it can be sliced and fried in e.v. olive oil.

Recommended wine
Montescudaio rosso

Minestra di fagioli
(Bean soup)

Ingredients
250 g dried haricot beans
(or fresh "borlotti")
350 g of winter cabbage
and savoy cabbage
2 carrots
1 stalk of celery
1 medium-sized onion
1 ham rind
2 ripe tomatoes
some basil leaves
1/2 cup of e.v. olive oil
8 slices of country-style brea

Soak the beans for 12 hours in abundant cold water. Discard the water, put the beans in a pot and add enough water to cook them; simmer over gentle heat with the ham rind.

Meanwhile clean and wash the cabbage, winter cabbage, carrot and celery, then slice them. Peel and chop the onion and sauté it gently in a pan with 2-3 tablespoons of oil.

Add the peeled and chopped tomatoes along with a few basil leaves. After a few minutes, add the cabbage, winter cabbage, carrot and celery and leave to stew gently.

When the vegetables are tender, add half the beans with a little of their cooking-water. Remove the ham rind and grind the remaining beans in a vegetable mill. Add this bean purée to the soup and simmer for an hour

over low heat. When done, taste for salt and pepper. Line a large serving bowl with bread slices and pour over them the boiling soup.

Continue with more layers of bread and soup. Leave to rest for a few moments before serving.

Recommended wine
Pomino rosso

Minestra di lenticchie
(Lentil soup)

Ingredients
250 g dried lentils
2 cloves of garlic
1 stalk of celery
1 sprig of sage
4 salted anchovy fillets
150 g peeled tomatoes
1 tablespoon butter
slices of country-style bread
grated parmesan
e.v. olive oil

For 16
1000gm lents
8 ~~10~~ garlic
4 celery
4 sage
16 anchovy
600g peeled toms
4 butter

Wash the lentils and soak them in cold water for at least 8 hours. Drain and put in a pot with fresh water. Bring to the boil, then simmer covered over gentle heat.

Meanwhile, chop the garlic and celery and sauté gently in a saucepan with a little oil. Wash the anchovies under running water to remove the salt, clean them, remove the scales and add to the well-browned vegetables, along with a few sage leaves. Put the peeled tomatoes through a sieve and add to the casserole. Cook for about 10 minutes.

When the lentils are done, add a little salt. Pour the lentils and their liquid into the pan with the other ingredients and simmer for 30 minutes. Season with salt and pepper.

In the meantime, fry the slices of bread in a pan with sizzling butter. Place them in individual soup bowls. Sprinkle with grated parmesan and ladle over them the lentil soup.

Seasoned it with a pinch of pepper and leave it to rest a few minutes before serving.

Recommended wine
Bianco Vergine Valdichiana

Minestra di lago
(Lake soup)

Ingredients

700 g fresh tench
1 medium-sized onion
2 cloves of garlic
a bunch of fresh parsley
1 glass of dry white wine
1 l of stock
200 g peeled tomatoes
1 carrot
1 potato
130 g rice or pasta for soups
e.v. olive oil

Clean the tench and wash it well, carefully removing all the scales, then cut it in pieces. In a pan, sauté, garlic, onion and plenty of finely chopped parsley in a little olive oil. Add the pieces of fish, stirring carefully. When the fish is lightly browned, add the white wine and stock. Reduce the liquid slightly over a rather hot flame, then add the chopped tomatoes, season with salt and pepper and cook at medium heat until the fish begins to come away from the bones. Then put it all through a sieve.

Clean the carrot and potato and cut into thin slices. Add them to the pureed mixture and return to the heat. When it comes to the boil add the rice or pasta and cook, taking care that the soup remains sufficiently liquid.

If necessary add some stock or hot water. Season to taste, add a drop of fresh olive oil and serve.

Recommended wine
Montescudaio rosso

Minestra di pane
(Bread soup)

Ingredients

650 g fresh "borlotti" beans
300 g peeled tomatoes
70 g pork rind
40 g bacon fat
1 piece of savoy cabbage
2 leaves of winter cabbage
2 stalks of celery
2 cloves of garlic
1 medium-sized onion
basil, parsley
slices of country-style bread
e.v. olive oil

Shell the beans and place them in a pot, preferably earthenware. Add abundant water, cover and simmer over low heat. When done, season with salt. In another pan, blanch the pork rind with the savoy and the winter cabbage for about 10 minutes. Meanwhile, chop the onion, celery, 1 clove of garlic, the parsley, basil and bacon fat and sauté in olive oil over a gentle heat.

When it begins to brown, add the chopped tomatoes and a pinch of pepper and cook for about 15 minutes. When done, pour into the pot with the beans. Then add the pork rind and the cabbage and winter cabbage cut into strips.

Stir with a wooden spoon and cook for an hour, until the pork rind is tender. Taste for salt.

Now toast the slices of country-style bread and rub them with the remaining clove of garlic. Place a layer of toasted bread in a terrine or large serving bowl and cover with the soup.

Continue with further layers until the ingredients are finished. Leave this delicious dish to rest for a few moments before serving.

Recommended wine
Montescudaio rosso

Minestra di zucca
(Pumpkin soup)

Ingredients
250 g yellow pumpkin
2 potatoes
1 medium-sized onion
1 l of stock (scant)
1 glass of milk (scant)
80 g spinach
1 tablespoon butter
grated parmesan
e.v. olive oil
white pepper
slices of country-style bread

First of all, try to find a fleshy pumpkin of the "lardaia" variety if possible, the best kind for this recipe. Then peel and finely chop the onion. Sauté it gently in a frying pan in a couple of tabletablespoons of oil. When it is golden, add the peeled, washed and sliced potatoes.

Clean the pumpkin, dice it and add it to the potatoes. Then let it absorb the flavours by cooking over a medium heat.

Transfer the pumpkin mixture to a saucepan. Cover with the stock and milk and simmer for 3/4 hour.

Meanwhile, clean, wash and boil the spinach in a little water. Drain it and chop it. When the pumpkin and the potatoes are done, put them through a sieve together with the chopped spinach.

Put the mixture back in the pan, add a tablespoon of butter and bring to the boil again, testing for salt and pepper.

In the meantime, toast the slices of bread in the oven. Place them in a serving bowl, pour the soup over them, and sprinkle with grated parmesan before serving.

Recommended wine
Rosato
di Carmignano

Minestrone toscano
(Tuscan vegetable soup)

Shell, wash and boil the beans. When done, drain them, retaining the cooking-water. Put half the beans through the sieve.

Finely chop the garlic, celery, onion, carrot, basil and place in a pan with the diced smoked bacon. Sauté in olive oil, stirring with a wooden spoon.

Clean and dice the other vegetables and add them together with the whole beans, the puréed beans and their liquid.

Add more hot water. Season with salt and pepper. Bring to the boil and then reduce the heat and simmer for about 30 minutes, protecting the bottom of the pan with a wire gauze heat spreader.

Serve the soup with slices of toasted bread, or, if you prefer, add small sized pasta to the soup as it boils; calculate the time according to the type of pasta.

Ingredients
300 g short pasta (or slices of toasted bread)
250 g fresh "borlotti" beans
150 g beet leaves
1 slice smoked bacon
1/2 savoy cabbage
1/2 winter cabbage
3 tomatoes
2 leeks
2 carrots
1 onion
1 stalk of celery
1 clove of garlic
fresh basil
e.v. olive oil

Recommended wine
Montecarlo rosso

Panzanella
(Cold bread salad)

Ingredients

350 g stale country-style bread
200 g fresh, not over-ripe tomatoes
2 fresh onions
1 cucumber
a bunch of basil
red wine vinegar
e.v. olive oil
white pepper

"Panzanella" is a traditional peasant dish which used to be eaten for breakfast or as a rustic snack. It can be served either as a first course or, in smaller quantities, as a starter.

Cut the stale bread into thick slices. Place them in a terrine. Cover with water and leave to rest for about 20 minutes.

Meanwhile, clean and wash the onions, basil, tomatoes and cucumber. Cut the vegetables into pieces and chop the basil. Place all this in a salad bowl. Drain the bread, squeeze it well, crumble it up and add it to the vegetables.

Recommended wine
Colline Lucchesi
rosso

Season with salt, white pepper, plenty of red wine vinegar (preferably flavoured with herbs) and oil. Stir well and leave to rest about 30 minutes before serving.

Pappa col pomodoro
(Bread and tomato soup)

Ingredients

700 g ripe tomatoes
300 g stale country-style bread
1 l of stock (light on salt)
3 cloves of garlic
1/2 cup of e.v. olive oil
6 basil leaves

This simple peasant recipe using leftover bread is undoubtedly one of the most famous Tuscan recipes. Its success depends more on the freshness of the ingredients used than on the culinary skills of the cook.

Wash the tomatoes well. Then cut them in pieces and cook in a saucepan over gentle heat. When done, put them through a sieve.

Then slice the stale bread and toast in the oven. In another pan heat up the stock, add the puréed toma-

toes, the toasted bread, oil, minced garlic, whole basil leaves, salt and pepper and cook gently stirring frequently with a wooden spoon until the consistency is thick but creamy.

Remove the basil leaves, taste for salt and pepper. Serve the soup, adding a dribbling of fresh olive oil.

Recommended wine
Chianti
Colline Pisane

Pasta e ceci
(Pasta and chick peas)

Ingredients
200 g dried chick peas
2 l of water
200 g "ditalini" pasta
200 g puréed tomatoes
2 cloves of garlic
1 sprig of rosemary
e.v. olive oil

Soak the chick peas in cold water for about 24 hours, then rinse and boil in 2 litres of water. When they are done, remove a few tablespoons and blend the rest with their cooking-water until smooth. Season with salt and stir well.

In the meantime, finely chop the garlic and rosemary, then sauté them in oil in a large pan. Add the puréed tomatoes. Add the chick peas, both the blended and the whole ones, and stir well. Bring to a boiling

Nepitella

"Nepitella", called also "nipitella" in Tuscany and calamint in English, has an aroma similar to that of mint. It grows profusely in cool, shady places, in forest clearings and fallow fields, up to the altitude of 1500 m.

The leaves and the flowery tips are used, picked at the moment when they blossom in summer, bound in loose bundles and left to dry in a shady, well-ventilated place.

They can also be used to flavour wine, by leaving 15 g of the plant to marinate in 1 l of sweet wine along with a stick of cinnamon, a pinch of vanilla and a few cloves. Leave the wine to rest for ten days, stirring from time to time, then strain it.

point and add the "ditalini" – pasta dried in tubular form about 1/2 cm in diameter and 1/2 cm long. (You can also use long pasta, such as "linguine", broken into pieces.)

As soon as the pasta is cooked, remove the soup from the heat and serve.

Recommended wine
Montescudaio rosso

Ribollita
(Twice-cooked vegetable soup)

Ingredients

150 g boiled white beans (or "cannellini")
150 g boiled haricot beans
250 g beet leaves
250 g winter cabbage
150 g spinach
150 g carrots
50 g celery
1 small onion
2 tablespoons of tomato purée
2 cloves of garlic
1 sprig of sage
1 sprig of rosemary
1 l of stock
150 g stale country-style bread
1,5 dl e.v. olive oil

Peel and finely chop the onion. Sauté in oil in a casserole, preferably earthenware. When browned, add the tomato purée and a ladleful of stock. Boil for a few minutes.

Clean, wash and chop the carrots and celery. Add them to the casserole and leave to stew over low heat. Clean and carefully wash the spinach, beet leaves and winter cabbage.

Chop them coarsely and stir in with the other ingredients, adding a little stock. Stew for 30 minutes over gentle heat, then add the beans with their cooking-water and simmer for another 1/2 hour.

Lastly, taste for salt and add a few tablespoons of hot oil in which the chopped garlic, sage and rosemary have been sauteed.

Cut the stale bread into thin slices. Place layers of bread in a large serving bowl, pouring soup over each layer. Leave to rest for a few hours.

Before serving, heat the soup up again in a casserole, crumbling it lightly with a wooden spoon, and season with a good pinch of pepper.

Recommended wine
Chianti Rufina

Zuppa di cardi (Cardoon soup)

Clean, rinse and dice the cardoons. Blanch them in lightly salted boiling water for a few minutes. Drain and leave to cool. Meanwhile heat the oil and butter in a pan. Add the chopped bacon-fat and onion and sauté gently. Dry the cardoons and coat them in flour. Add them to the sauteed onion and braise them for a few minutes. Add a little stock and simmer for a good 30 minutes. Then put the soup through a sieve and return to a gentle heat. Add another tablespoon of butter: Taste for salt and pepper and leave to simmer for a few more minutes. In the meantime, toast the slices of bread in a pan greased with butter. Put them in a large serving bowl and pour the boiling soup over them. Leave to rest for a few moments before serving, to let the bread soften.

Recommended wine
Rosso di Montalcino

Zuppa di funghi alla lucchese ▶▶
(Mushroom soup Lucca-style)

Ingredients

300 g mushrooms
1/2 celery stalk
1/2 onion
1 clove garlic
2 tablespoons puréed tomatoes
1 tablespoon freshly chopped parsley
1 l of stock
grated parmesan
e.v. olive oil
4 slices country-style bread

Clean and gently sauté the finely chopped vegetables (except for the parsley) in a little oil. Add the mushrooms, cleaned, washed, dried and diced, and cook for 10 minutes. Then add the puréed tomatoes and 2 full cups of hot stock. Add the chopped parsley and leave to simmer for about 30 minutes, adding more stock if the soup is too thick. When done, sprinkle generously with grated parmesan. Place the lightly toasted slices of bread in individual bowls, pour the soup over them and serve.

Recommended wine
Bianco di Pitigliano

Zuppa di cavolo nero
(Winter cabbage soup)

Ingredients

500 g winter cabbage
50 g streaky bacon
1 small onion
1 clove of garlic
2-3 tablespoons of
e.v. olive oil
4 large slices of countrystyle
bread
grated pecorino (optional)
whole black pepper

Clean and wash the cabbage, detaching the leaves. Chop the onion, garlic and bacon and sauté in a pan with 2-3 tablespoons of oil. Add the cabbage leaves. Cover and simmer for a few minutes over gentle heat. Then add some lightly salted water and simmer for at least 1 hour. Meanwhile toast the bread and place in a large serving bowl.

Sprinkle with grated pecorino according to taste and a good pinch of black pepper. When the soup is ready, pour it gently into a serving bowl. Leave to rest for a few moments before serving.

Recommended wine

*Chianti
di Montalbano*

Pasta and rice

Cappelletti saporiti
(Tasty fresh pasta)

Prepare the fresh pasta [see basic recipe, p. 34] and let it rest. Clean the chard and blanch in boiling salted water. Drain and press out the excess moisture, then blend. Now put the chard in a bowl and add the grated parmesan, the eggs, a pinch of salt, pepper and nutmeg, mixing well. Using a pastry wheel, cut the pasta into 3 cm squares.

Put a little filling on each. Then fold them diagonally into triangles. Seal the edges with your fingers. At this point, join the two opposite corners of the triangle and press them between your thumb and forefinger. Leave to rest for a few hours.

In the meantime, prepare the sauce. Wash the chicken livers and chop them coarsely. Sauté the onion and rosemary in the oil until golden.

Add the liver and bay leaf and sauté, sprinkling with the white wine.

Season with salt and pepper. When the wine has evaporated, add the tomato sauce [see basic recipe, p. 45] and finish cooking over moderate heat.

Cook the cappelletti in salted water, putting them in the water just as it is coming to the boil. When they are done, drain and pour into a bowl. Add the sauce, sprinkle with grated parmesan and serve.

Ingredients
rolled fresh pasta dough
FILLING:
250 g chard
250 g grated parmesan
2 eggs
nutmeg
SAUCE:
200 g chicken liver
1 spring onion
2 tablespoons of tomato
  sauce
1 sprig of fresh rosemary
2 bay leaves
1 glass of white wine
grated parmesan
e.v. olive oil

Recommended wine
Montecarlo rosso

Fresh Pasta

Ingredienti

400 g of wheat flour, type 00	1 tablespoon of e.v. olive oil
4 eggs	salt

The pasta dough can be also be prepared without the addition of oil and salt and can contain a different quantity of eggs, according to the recipe. Some cooks believe in using one egg for every 100 g of flour, others increase these proportions, and still others decrease it. But all of them agree that the room where the pasta is made should not be too cold, nor should it be exposed to draughts, which would have a negative effect on the procedure.

Pour the flour in a cone on the counter, leaving a slight depression in the middle, like a crater. Break the eggs into the crater one by one, and begin to stir in the flour from around the edges. Continue to stir the flour into the eggs, adding the oil and the salt. Continue to mix, first delicately with the fingertips, then more vigourously as the mixture becomes thicker. Always keep the liquid part of the eggs inside the cone of flour until it has been fully amalgamated. A little warm water is sometimes added, but only if really necessary. The end result should be a dough that is smooth and even, which you will form into a ball. At this point, there are two possibilities. The first is that of bringing the dough immediately to the 'breaking point', by kneading it until it begins to swell here and there, as if it were alive, forming air bubbles. In this case, it is preferable to divide it into two or or more parts, then to roll each part flat with a rolling-pin, knead it again and then roll it flat again until it reaches the ideal thickness of 1-2 mm. Let the sheets of rolled dough rest at least 30 minutes on a floured cloth, then fold them and cut them into the desired pasta format.

The second possibility consists of kneading the dough a little less and forming it into a single ball which is left to rest, under a barely damp cloth, for about 30 minutes. The dough is then divided, roll out into sheets and used as pasta to be filled.

Gnocchetti alla fiorentina
(Spinach and potato dumplings)

Ingredients
1 kg potatoes
300 g spinach
200 g wheat flour
1 egg
SAUCE:
butter
sage
grated parmesan

Peel the potatoes and boil in salted water. Meanwhile, clean the spinach thoroughly and boil in salted water. When done, press out the excess moisture and put through a sieve. When the potatoes are cooked, drain and mash.

Blend the spinach and potatoes together, incorporating an egg. Add the flour and continue to mix. If the dough is too soft, add more flour to obtain the right consistency.

Form the dough into long tubes and then cut it into 2 cm pieces; place them on a floured cloth. Then plunge them into boiling salted water. As soon as they come to the surface, remove them out with a perforated spoon, draining well, and place in a serving bowl.

Serve them with butter melted with sage leaves and a generous helping of grated parmesan.

Recommended wine
Elba rosso

Pannicelli
(Fresh filled pasta)

Ingredients
rolled fresh pasta dough
1.5 l of chicken stock
FILLING:
300 g fresh ricotta
200 g boiled beet leaves
100 g boiled spinach
100 g bland dry pecorino
  (grated)
nutmeg
SAUCE:
tomato sauce
grated pecorino
butter

Prepare fresh pasta dough [see basic recipe, previous page], roll it out with a rolling-pin and cut it into rectangles of approx. 8 x 15 cm. Place them, well separated, on a cloth.

Bring the chicken stock to a boil.

Meanwhile, chop the boiled beet leaves and spinach together and mix in the crumbled ricotta. Season with salt, pepper, nutmeg and grated pecorino, mixing well.

When the stock reaches the boiling point, cook the pannicelli in it for a few minutes. When done, drain them and place them in a an ovenproof dish, covering each layer with some of the greens and grated pecorino mixture. Conclude with a layer of tomato sauce [see basic recipe, p. 45], a sprinkling of pecorino and a few dabs of butter.

Place in an oven preheated to around 180 °C, gratinate for 15 minutes, then remove from the oven and wait a few minutes before serving.

Recommended wine
Chianti Rufina

Pappardelle al cervo e porcini ▶▶
(Pappardelle in venison and mushroom sauce)

Ingredients
400 g pappardelle
350 g lean venison
150 g cep mushrooms
1/2 l red wine
1 spring onion
1 small carrot
2 bay leaves
1 sprig of rosemary
40 g of butter
grated parmesan

Prepare the pappardelle [see basic recipe, p. 38] and set them aside. Dice the venison and marinate it in the red wine with the whole herbs, the onion and the carrot for about 12 hours. Remove and drain the meat. Then drain the vegetables and herbs. Chop them and sauté them in sizzling butter in a large saucepan.

Clean, wash delicately and dry the mushrooms. Cut them in thin slices and wilt them in butter in a separate pan. Add the diced venison to the sauteed vegetables and brown rapidly for a few minutes, sprinkling with a glass of red wine. Season with salt and pepper. Turn the heat down, cover and cook for about 1/2 an hour stirring occasionally. Lastly, add the mushrooms.

At this point, cook the pasta in a large pot of boiling salted water. Drain when still al dente and add to the sauce. Cook rapidly for a few minutes and serve with the grated parmesan.

Recommended wine
Nobile
di Montepulciano

36

Pappardelle al fagiano
(Pappardelle with pheasant sauce)

Ingredients
400 g pappardelle
1/2 pheasant
1 small glass of cognac
1 glass of dry white wine
1 cup of vegetable stock
a bunch of fresh sage
a sprig of rosemary
60 g butter
1 tablespoon of cream
grated parmesan

Prepare the pappardelle [see basic recipe] and set them aside.

Clean the pheasant and remove the bones. Cut into strips and sauté until golden with a few sage leaves in 30 g of butter.

Sprinkle with the cognac, then the white wine and cook until they evaporate. Reduce the heat, cover and cook for about 1/2 hour, occasionally adding some hot stock.

Remove the strips of pheasant and strain the juices. In a separate pan, melt the remaining butter with the rosemary.

Put the meat and the strained juices back in the pan, adding the butter flavoured with rosemary.

PAPPARDELLE, TAGLIATELLE AND TAGLIOLINI

Ingredients
500 g of flour type 00
4 eggs

1 tablespoon e.v. olive oil
1/2 cup of maize flour

These are prepared exactly the same as sheets of fresh past dough [see basic recipe, p. 34], up to the step in which sheets of pasta 1-2 mm thick have been rolled out.

Let the sheets of pasta rest about 30 minutes on a floured cloth or table, sprinkling them with a little maize flour. Then fold them and cut them with a knife into ribbons of the desired width, to obtain pappardelle, tagliatelle or tagliolini, more or less from 2 cm to 5 mm wide.

Cook the pasta in a large pot of boiling salted water. Drain while still al dente and add to the pheasant sauce. Add the cream and mix well. Serve the pappardelle with a generous sprinkling of grated parmesan.

Recommended wine
Nobile
di Montepulciano

Pappardelle sul cinghiale
(Pappardelle with wild boar sauce)

Ingredients
400 g pappardelle
200 g puréed tomatoes
100 g minced wild boar
4 cloves of garlic
1 stalk of celery
2 cloves, 2 bay leaves
1 sprig of rosemary
1/2 glass of red wine
1 cup of stock
grated parmesan
hot red pepper
e.v. olive oil

Prepare the pappardelle [see basic recipe, p. 38] and set them aside. Finely chop all the herbs and sauté gently in the oil with the whole cloves of garlic. When the garlic starts to turn golden add the meat, stirring it to absorb the flavours. Season with salt and after a few minutes add the red wine. When the wine has evaporated, add the puréed tomatoes and cook over low heat for about 2 hours, adding a little stock from time to time to keep the sauce from drying. Boil the pappardelle in a large pot of salted water, drain when done and place in a serving bowl. Dress them with the sauce and a good sprinkling of grated parmesan.

Recommended wine
Brunello
di Montalcino

Pici al pomodoro e ricotta salata
(Pici in tomato and ricotta sauce)

Ingredients
400 g pici
4 ripe tomatoes
1 leek
1 bunch of fresh basil
aged salted ricotta cheese
e.v. olive oil

Prepare the pici [see basic recipe, p. 40]. Peel the tomatoes, after having briefly plunged them in boiling water to loosen the skins, and cut them into strips. Clean the leek well, using only the tender white part, and slice it thinly. Heat oil in a saucepan and sauté the leek until golden. Add the strips of tomato and a pinch of salt and cook until it reduces slightly. Cook the pasta in a large pot of boiling salted water. Drain when still "al dente" and add to the sauce. Cook for a 1 minute, stirring all the time. Sprinkle with a helping of grated salted ricotta. Add a pinch of pepper and chopped basil.

Recommended wine
Montescudaio rosso

Pici all'aglione (Pici in garlic sauce)

Ingredients
400 g pici
40 g fresh garlic
700 g peeled tomatoes
50 g grated pecorino
e.v. olive oil

Prepare the pici [see basic recipe]. Then peel the garlic. Chop it into slices and put it in an earthenware pot with plenty of oil. Sauté over a gentle heat. Wash, peel and sieve the tomatoes, after having briefly plunged them into boiling water to loosen the skins, then add them to the pot. Season with salt and pepper and cook for 30 minutes over gentle heat. Cook the pasta in a large pot of boiling salted water. Drain when still "al dente". Put it in a large bowl with the hot sauce and serve at once. Serve the grated pecorino separately.

Recommended wine
Bolgheri rosato

Pɪcɪ

Ingredients
400 g of flour type 0 or 00   salt
1 tablespoon of e.v. olive oil   water

Pour the flour onto the rolling board and add the oil, a pinch of salt and enough water to form a smooth, elastic dough. Knead well. Cover with a cloth and let rest for 20 minutes. Then roll out the dough to form a sheet about 1.5 cm thick, using a rolling-pin. Cut the sheet of pasta into ribbons 3 mm thin.
Coat your hands with flour and roll the strips to round them into shape.

Pici con carciofi e olive
(Pici with artichokes and olives)

Ingredients
400 g pici
8 artichoke hearts
12 black olives
4 ripe tomatoes
1 clove of garlic
1 sprig of fresh rosemary
1 lemon
aged pecorino
1/2 cup e.v. olive oil

Prepare the pici [see basic recipe, p. 40]. Finely chop the rosemary needles and sauté until golden in the oil with the garlic. Meanwhile, clean the artichokes retaining only the hearts. Put them in a bowl of water to which lemon juice has been added, to keep them from turning brown. Then cut them in quarters and add them to the pan, along with the stoned black olives, previously sautéed in a separate pan, and the tomatoes, peeled (after having been briefly plunged into boiling water), chopped, and with the seeds discarded.

Season with salt and pepper and cook over a medium heat, stirring frequently with a wooden spoon.

Cook the pasta in a large pot of boiling salted water. Drain while still al dente and add to the sauce. Stir to mix well all the ingredients. Sprinkle with the grated pecorino and serve.

Recommended wine
Bianco di Pitigliano

Pici con piselli
(Pici in pea sauce)

Ingredients
400 g pici
300 g fresh shelled peas
30 g butter
1 tablespoon of mascarpone
aged salted ricotta
nutmeg

Prepare the pici [see basic recipe, p. 40]. Cook the peas gently in the butter, just long enough to barely soften them.

Cook the pasta in a large pot of boiling salted water. Drain while still al dente and add to the peas. Add the mascarpone. Sprinkle with the grated ricotta. Season with a little nutmeg. When all the ingredients have been well amalgamated, serve.

Recommended wine
Bianco di Pitigliano

Pici con rigaglie
(Pici in giblet sauce)

First prepare the pici [see basic recipe, p. 40]. Then clean and wash the chicken giblets. Dry them and chop into pieces.

Mince together the parsley, bacon, white part of the leek and rosemary needles and sauté them in oil till golden. Add the giblets. Sprinkle with the white wine and cook till it evaporates.

Clean, wash, dry and slice the mushrooms. Add them to the giblets together with the tomato purée. Cook over a medium heat stirring frequently with a wooden spoon.

Cook the pasta in a large pot of boiling salted water. Drain and add to the sauce, stirring well. Sprinkle with grated parmesan and pepper.

Ingredients
400 g pici
150 g chicken giblets
100 g mushrooms
   (Cantharellus cibarius)
1 thick slice of bacon
2 tablespoons of tomato
   purée
1 glass of dry white wine
1 bunch of fresh parsley
1 leek
1 sprig of fresh rosemary
grated parmesan
e.v. olive oil

Recommended wine
Parrina rosso

Pici con uova di luccio
(Pici with pike roe)

The best time to prepare this recipe is between mid-February and the beginning of May, when the pike are ready to reproduce.

Prepare the pici [see basic recipe, p. 40]. Wash, dry and chop some of the parsley. Sauté it gently in a pan with a little oil. Wash, peel and chop the fresh tomatoes (after having briefly plunged them into boiling water to loosen the skins).

Peel and finely chop the onion. Add the tomatoes and onion to the pan with the parsley and cook for a few

Ingredients
400 g pici
200 g fresh pike roe
1 medium-sized onion
200 g fresh tomatoes
1 hot red pepper
1 bunch of fresh parsley
1/2 glass of white wine
2 tablespoons of e.v. olive oil

minutes over medium heat. Then add the pike roe, the hot red pepper and a pinch of salt. Sprinkle with a little white wine and continue to cook over very gentle heat.

Cook the pasta in a large pot of boiling salted water. Drain when still "al dente" and place in a serving dish. Add the sauce and a handful of chopped parsley, then serve.

Recommended wine
Bianco di Pitigliano

Ravioloni di asparagi
(Ravioli filled with asparagus)

Ingredients
fresh pasta dough
FILLING:
250 g asparagus tips
100 g fresh ricotta
100 g grated parmesan
1 egg
SAUCE:
40 g butter
1 sprig of fresh rosemary
grated parmesan

Prepare sheets of dough for ravioli [see basic recipe, p. 34]. Then prepare the filling.

Wash and clean the asparagus, using the tips only. Scald them in steam and set aside 20 of them for the sauce. Chop the rest of the asparagus and blend with the ricotta, grated parmesan and egg in a bowl. Season with salt and pepper. Mix well and place heaps of the filling the size of a walnut on half the sheet of pasta. Fold the over half over it and press it down with your fingers around each heap of filling. Then cut the pasta into 4 cm squares, using a knife or a pastry cutter.

Melt the butter in a pan with the rosemary and sautée gently. In a separate pan, cook the remaining asparagus tips in a little butter until tender.

Cook the ravioloni in a large pot of salted water. Drop them in the water just as it is coming to the boil. When they are done, drain well, place in a large serving bowl and add the melted butter and the asparagus tips. Sprinkle with grated parmesan before serving.

Recommended wine
Bolgheri bianco

Ravioloni di zucchine
(Ravioli filled with courgettes)

Ingredients
fresh pasta dough
FILLING:
200 g courgettes
150 g fresh ricotta
100 g grated parmesan
nutmeg
butter
SAUCE:
tomato sauce
butter
grated parmesan
a few leaves of fresh basil

Prepare sheets of dough for ravioli [see basic recipe, p. 34]. Clean, wash, dry and finely slice the courgettes. Cook until tender in a little butter, seasoning with salt and nutmeg. Put them through a sieve and blend with the ricotta and the grated parmesan in a bowl. Make the ravioloni, by placing heaps of filling the size of a walnut on one half of the pasta. Fold the other half over and press it down around each heap of filling with your fingers. Using a pastry wheel, cut it into 4 cm squares. Cook the ravioloni in a large pot of salted water. When done, drain well, transfer to a serving dish and add a little melted butter and tomato sauce [see basic recipe]. Stir, garnish with chopped basil, sprinkle with grated parmesan and serve.

Recommended wine
*Bianco
della Valdinievole*

TOMATO SAUCE

Ingredients

500 g tomatoes	1 clove of garlic
1 carrot	1 bunch of fresh basil
1 onion	whole black pepper
1 stalk of celery	e.v. olive oil

Wash the tomatoes, peel them after plunging them briefly into boiling water to loosen the skins, and slice them. Cut the onion into fine slices and chop the celery and carrots. Heat a few tablespoons of olive oil in a saucepan and sauté all of the ingredients with the clove of garlic and a few basil leaves. Season with oil, salt and freshly-ground black pepper. Stir and simmer at moderate heat until the vegetables are tender. At this point, remove the garlic and basil leaves and strain the sauce.

Rigatoni di San Miniato
(Rigatoni of San Miniato)

Ingredients

400 g rigatoni
200 g puréed tomatoes
150 g minced beef
50 g bacon
4 chicken livers
1/2 glass of dry white wine
1 onion
1 carrot
1 clove of garlic
2 fresh sage leaves
2 fresh basil leaves
2 tablespoons chopped parsley
1 sprig of rosemary
1 cup of stock
grated parmesan
e.v. olive oil

Recommended wine

Bianco Vergine Valdichiana

Finely chop all the herbs, using just a few rosemary needles and sauté them in an earthenware pot in a little oil. Wash the chicken livers and chop them up with the bacon. Add to the herbs together with the minced beef and stir well. Cook for a few minutes to soak up the flavours and then add the white wine and cook until it evaporates. Season with salt and a good sprinkling of freshly ground pepper. Add the puréed tomatoes. Mix well, cover and cook over gentle heat for at least 2 hours. If the sauce tends to dry up, add a little hot stock.

Boil the pasta in abundant salted water. Drain when al dente and pour into the pan with the sauce. Stir over the flame for a few minutes. Serve with grated parmesan.

Riso con coratella d'agnello
(Rice with lamb interior)

Ingredients

400 g rice type "Vialone nano"
pluck from 1 lamb
200 g fresh tomatoes
100 g butter
1 medium-sized onion
fresh parsley
1.5 l of stock
2 lemons
1 bunch of parsley

Finely chop the onion and parsley together and sautè them in a pan with the butter.

Cut the lamb interior into small pieces separating the lungs from the heart and the liver. Add the coarsely chopped lungs to the pan and continue to cook, adding a little stock.

After a few minutes, add the chopped heart. When it begins to brown, add the chopped liver. When this has browned, add the tomatoes (peeled after having been briefly plunged into boiling water to loosen the skins) and season with salt and pepper.

Meanwhile, cook the rice in the stock for 12 minutes and then drain. Stir in the remaining butter, transfer it to a casserole and put it in a hot oven (200 °C) for 10 minutes.

Add the lemon juice to the sauce and continue to cook uncovered over gentle heat. Remove the rice from the oven, make sure it is nice and dry and place it in the centre of a serving dish.

Arrange the sauce around it. Sprinkle with chopped parsley.

Recommended wine
Parrina rosso

Risotto al tartufo
(Risotto with truffles)

Ingredients
400 g rice type "Arborio" or "Carnaroli"
1 black truffle
1 l of stock
60 g butter
50 g grated parmesan
1 glass sparkling white wine
1 onion

Peel and finely slice the onion. Cook it in a little olive oil in an earthenware pan until just tender. Add the rice and sauté for a few minutes before sprinkling it with the wine.

When the wine has evaporated, gradually add the boiling stock and continue to cook. In the meantime, brush the truffle well. Cut part of it into very thin flakes with a truffle-cutter and grate the rest. When the rice is nearly done, add the parmesan, the grated truffle and the soft butter and mix well. Remove the pan from the heat and cover it with a cloth. Leave to rest for a few minutes.

Serve with a sprinkling of flaked truffle and additional grated parmesan.

Recommended wine
Bianco Vergine
Valdichiana

Risotto alla toscana
(Risotto Tuscan-style)

Ingredients
400 g rice type "Arborio" "or Carnaroli"
50 g minced beef
50 g chicken liver and gizzard
1 onion
1 carrot
1 stalk of celery
1 cup of tomato purée
1 l of stock
1/2 glass of Chianti
grated parmesan
e.v. olive oil

Chop half an onion, the carrot and celery and fry in a few tablespoons of oil. Add the minced beef, the chopped chicken gizzard and after a couple of minutes the chopped liver. Add the wine and cook until it's nearly all evaporated. Then add a little tomato purée diluted in the warm stock. Season with salt and pepper and cook for a few minutes before removing from the heat. In another pan, fry the other chopped 1/2 onion in a little oil. Add the rice and stir with a wooden spoon until it has absorbed the oil. Season with salt and continue cooking, gradually adding the boiling stock and stirring all the time.

When it is ready, add the meat and liver sauce to the rice and mix well. Remove from the heat and leave to rest a few minutes with the lid on. Serve the grated parmesan separately.

Recommended wine
Montescudaio rosso

Risotto con ragù di piccione
(Risotto in pigeon ragout)

Ingredients
350 g rice type "Arborio"
1 pigeon
1 salted anchovy fillet
1 small black truffle
1 small onion
1 bay leaf
1 sprig of rosemary
1 piece of lemon rind
1 small glass of marsala
1 l litre of stock
grated parmesan
butter
e.v. olive oil

Clean and singe the pigeon. Chop the anchovy (rinsed and scaled), lemon rind (only the yellow part), and the rosemary needles. Add the bay leaf and use to stuff the pigeon. Place it in an ovenproof dish, season it with oil, salt and pepper and cook it in a hot oven (200 °C) for 20 minutes.

When it is cool, bone and chop the meat into strips (setting aside the giblets). Put the bones and the giblets back into the roasting tin with the cooking juices. Add a couple of ladlefuls of stock and a little of the marsala. Put back in the hot oven for about 10 minutes. Then remove the pigeon from the oven, keeping it warm, and strain the sauce, keeping it warm too.

Clean and chop the onion and sauté in a little oil in a casserole. Add the rice and, stirring constantly with a wooden spoon, cook until it has absorbed all the oil. At this point, add the remaining marsala and cook until it evaporates. Finish cooking the rice, adding a little stock at a time; 5 minutes before it is ready, add the pigeon meat and its sauce. Remove from the heat. Add grated parmesan and a tablespoon of butter and leave to rest for a few minutes with the lid on.

Clean the truffle and flake it with a truffle-cutter. Just before serving, stir the rice again and add the flaked truffle.

Recommended wine
*Rosso
di Montepulciano*

Risotto con vongole e fave
(Risotto with clams and broad beans)

Wash the clams and heat them in a covered pan with a little oil and the clove of garlic until the shells open. As they open, take them out of the pan and remove some of them from the shells. Then strain the liquid in the pan and reserve it.

Shell the beans and boil them for about 10 minutes in salted water, then remove their skins.

Cook the cleaned, chopped leeks (white part only) in a little oil until tender. Add the rice and stir well. Add the wine and then the liquid in which the clams were

Ingredients
350 g rice type "Arborio" or "Carnaroli"
800 g clams
800 g fresh broad beans
200 g leeks
1 clove of garlic
1 bunch of parsley
1 l of fish stock (or vegetable stock)
1/2 glass of dry white wine
e.v. olive oil

cooked, gradually stirring in the fish (or vegetable) stock (dried stock cubes can also be used); 10 minutes before the risotto is done, add the clams and the beans. Season with oil and chopped parsley. Leave to rest for a few minutes before serving.

Recommended wine
Bianco della Valdinievole

Risotto verde
(Green risotto)

Ingredients
400 g rice type "Arborio" or "Carnaroli"
200 g beet leaves
100 g butter
70 g grated parmesan
1 l of stock
1 medium-sized onion
nutmeg

Clean and wash the beet leaves. Boil for a few minutes, drain and put through a sieve to obtain a smooth purée. Melt one tablespoon of butter in a pot, preferably earthenware. Stir in the purée with a wooden spoon and leave near the flame. Melt the remaining butter in a casserole and gently sauté the peeled and chopped onion till golden. Add the rice and sauté it, stirring. Add some beef stock and season with salt and a pinch of nutmeg. Continue cooking and stirring, gradually adding hot stock. About 5 minutes before the rice is cooked, stir in the beet leaf purée, adding extra stock if necessary. When done, sprinkle with abundant grated parmesan, stir and serve.

Recommended wine
Montescudaio rosso

Spaghetti al tartufo nero
(Spaghetti in black truffle sauce)

Ingredients
400 g spaghetti
200 g black truffles
80 g salted anchovy fillets
1/2 clove of garlic
2 tablespoons of fresh chopped parsley
e.v. olive oil

Brush and grate the truffles. Crush the peeled garlic, anchovies, chopped parsley and truffles in a mortar to make a smooth paste. Dilute with a little oil and set aside while you cook the spaghetti in boiling salted water. When the pasta is done, pour it into a serving bowl. Heat the sauce without bringing it to the boil. Pour the sauce onto the pasta and serve with grated parmesan.

Recommended wine
Bianco di Pitigliano

Tortelli di cavolfiore
(Pasta filled with cauliflower)

Sauté the garlic and rosemary in a little oil. Then add the meat and the sausage broken into pieces. Season with salt and pepper.

Clean and wash the cauliflower. Parboil for 10 minutes in salted water. Then cut it in pieces and add it to the meat. When the cauliflower is well done, remove from the heat and add the egg yolks, beating vigorously in order to incorporate them in the mixture, which must be soft but firm.

To prepare the pasta for the tortelli, pour the flour in a cone on the pastry board. Add a little salt and the eggs. Knead patiently until little air bubbles form on the surface of the pasta.

Now roll the pasta into a ball, cover with a cloth and leave to rest for 30 minutes before rolling it out with a rolling pin. Cut the pasta into squares and place a tablespoon of the barely warm filling at the centre of each.

Fold the squares over diagonally to form triangles. Boil in a large panful of salted water. Serve with the melted butter and grated parmesan.

Ingredients
PASTA:
300 g flour
3 eggs
salt
FILLING:
250 g minced lean pork
250 g sausage
1/2 cauliflower
2 cloves of garlic
2 eggs
1 sprig of rosemary
pepper
SAUCE:
butter
grated parmesan

Recommended wine
Montescudaio rosso

Eggs

Ciancinfricola

Ingredients

8 eggs
1 clove of garlic
1 small onion
2 ripe tomatoes
1/2 cup of stock
e.v. olive oil

"Ciancinfricola" (or rather, "ciancinfri'ola") is a word deriving from dialect verbs "cianciare" and "sfricolare", and it conveys a very good idea of what goes on in the midst of a general 'cook-up', where the recipe calls for everything to be mixed and thrown in together.

Peel the garlic and onion, chop and sauté gently with a little oil in a pot, preferably earthenware, stirring with a wooden spoon, then add the well washed and chopped tomatoes (peeled after having briefly plunged them into boiling water to loosen the skins) as well as a tablespoon of stock. Season with salt and pepper, and cook over low heat until the tomato is almost entirely dry. Meanwhile beat the eggs in a bowl and them pour into the pot with the reduced tomato sauce; mix vigorously and cook until the eggs have absorbed all the sauce.

Recommended wine
Montescudaio rosso

Frittata al tartufo
(Omelette with truffles)

Ingredients

8 eggs
1 small black truffle
2 tablespoons grated parmesan
e.v. olive oil

Brush the truffle and grate half of it. Beat the eggs in a bowl, add the parmesan and the grated truffle, season with salt and pepper. Then heat a little oil in a shallow pan and pour the eggs in, allowing the omelette to cook without turning or flipping, so that it remains creamy on the surface. When it is done, slide it delicately onto the warmed serving dish, being careful not to overturn it. Lastly, dust it with the remaining portion of the truffle, sliced with a truffle-slicer.

Recommended wine
Bianco Vergine
Valdichiana

Frittata agli aromi
(Omelette with herbs)

Ingredients
8 eggs
300 g puréed tomatoes
1/2 carrot
1/2 onion
1/2 stalk celery
1 tablespoon chopped
  parsley
1 tablespoon flour
e.v. olive oil
whole black pepper
country-style bread

Thoroughly beat the eggs in a bowl together with the flour, salt and freshly milled pepper. Heat some oil in a medium-sized frying pan (the frittata should be about 1/2 cm thick) and pour the eggs into it. Cook the omelette on both sides. Then slide it onto a cutting board and cut it into medium-sized cubes. Grease the frying pan again and sauté the chopped onion, celery and carrot. When the vegetables are wilted, add the puréed tomatoes and parsley, season with salt and pepper, and cook for 15 minutes before adding the diced omelette to the sauce. Mix gently, allow to become imbued with the fragrances for a few minutes, then remove from heat. Serve with rounds of toasted bread.

Recommended wine
Montecarlo rosso

Frittata con gli zoccoli
(Omelette with clogs)

Ingredients
8 eggs
70 g thick-sliced cured ham
1 tablespoon butter
2 tablespoons e.v. olive oil

Beat up the eggs in a bowl, add salt and pepper. Cut the cured ham in little squares (thereby creating the so-called "clogs") and sauté them in a pan with a small quantity of oil and a tablespoon of butter. Sauté over moderate heat, mixing with a wooden spoon, then add the beaten eggs and proceed as for an ordinary omelette.

Recommended wine
Bolgheri rosato

Frittata alla porcara
(Swineherd's omelette)

Ingredients
8 eggs
slices of Sienese black pudding
or "buristo"
1 tablespoon flour
1/2 lemon
e.v. olive oil

Recommended wine
Chianti Colli Senesi

Flour the slices of buristo, arrange in a shallow pan with a dribble of hot oil, and brown lightly on both sides. Meanwhile beat the eggs in a bowl, add a few drops of lemon juice, season with salt and pepper. When the fat of the buristo begins to melt, add the beaten eggs and proceed as for a normal omelette.

Buristo

Also called "biroldo" in Tuscany, "buristo" is the typical Sienese blood pudding, made of pig's blood and lard seasoned with salt, pepper, mixed spices and cinnamon, packed in natural gut and aged for a brief time.
In Valdichiana it is customary to add raisins and pin nuts.

Frittata in trippa
(Omelette in tripe)

Ingredients
8 eggs
250 g puréed tomatoes
1 onion
1 tablespoon chopped parsley
grated parmesan
butter
e.v. olive oil

Beat the eggs together with 2 tablespoons of parmesan, the parsley and a pinch of salt, then prepare a number of thin pancake-type omelettes using a small frying pan greased with butter. Set aside. Meanwhile, after peeling and finely slicing the onion, wilt it in a wide pan with a little heated oil. As soon as the onion softens, pour the puréed tomatoes into the frying pan and cook slowly for 15 minutes. Roll up the pancakes on a wooden board and slice as if they were tagliatelle of pasta. Put them back in the tomato sauce for another 15 minutes, to absorb the flavour. Serve with a dusting of grated parmesan.

Recommended wine
Bolgheri rosato

Fish

Acciughe fritte
(Fried anchovies)

Ingredients
500 g fresh anchovies
1 small glass of vinegar
2 eggs
1 cup of flour
2 lemons
e.v. olive oil

Wash the anchovies with water and vinegar, wash, open into two halves, de-scale and rinse, then dry with a teacloth. Beat the eggs in a bowl with a pinch of salt, dip the anchovies in holding them by the tail, then coat them with flour and place immediately in a pan with sizzling hot oil. Gently brown the fish on both sides, blot off the excess oil rapidly with kitchen roll and serve immediately, garnished with lemon slices.

Recommended wine
Bianco di Pitigliano

Acciughe in teglia
(Anchovies in a pan)

Ingredients
500 g fresh anchovies
2 cloves of garlic
1 tablespoon chopped parsley
1/2 lemon
e.v. olive oil

Wash the anchovies carefully with water and vinegar, then clean, open into two halves, de-scale, rinse and dry on a clean cloth.

Bianco di Pitigliano

This white wine, which takes its name from the town in the Province of Grosseto, is produced on land of volcanic origin, which extends from the Lake of Bolsena as far as the town of Pitigliano. In colour it is straw-yellow with brilliant greenish reflections; it has a delicate bouquet; dry, neutral flavour with a slight bitterish aftertaste, of medium body, soft. It is best when served cold, at 10 °C, with soups, seafood dishes and appetizers.

Peel and lightly sauté the garlic with a little oil in a shallow pan, then add the anchovies, browning on both sides. Add the chopped parsley, then remove from heat and sprinkle the fish with lemon juice.

Recommended wine
*Bianco Pisano
di San Torpè*

Anguilla in zimino
(Eel in samin sauce)

Ingredients
1 eel, about 1 kg
500 g puréed tomatoes
300 g fresh peas
1 onion
1 tablespoon chopped
  parsley
hot red pepper
e.v. olive oil

Clean the eel discarding the head and the interior and cut into pieces about 4 cm long. Gently sauté the peeled chopped onion with a the crumbled hot red pepper. As soon as they are wilted, add the chopped parsley and the eel, browned lightly, then add the puréed tomatoes.

Cook for about 1/2 hour. Remove the eel from the pan, keeping it warm. Put the shelled fresh peas in the same pan and cook until done. When the peas are tender, return the eel to the pan, mix delicately for a few minutes to blend the flavours, then serve.

Recommended wine
Montescudaio rosso

Aringhe con polenta
(Herrings with polenta)

Ingredients
4 smoked herrings
300 g of cornmeal
300 g grated pecorino
200 g sliced bacon fat
vinegar
e.v. olive oil

Prepare the polenta [see basic recipe, p. 58]. When it has cooked for 30 minutes add to it the slices of bacon fat, after having briefly cooked them on a hot griddle pan, continuing to stir well to mix them evenly with the polenta.

Cook for another 10-15 minutes, then pour the polenta onto a cutting board onto a counter where it can cool. Meanwhile wash the herrings and broil them lightly. Cut them in pieces and dress with oil and vinegar. Slice the cooled polenta, place a piece of herring on each slice and sprinkle with grated pecorino.

Recommended wine
Bolgheri bianco

Baccalà alla livornese
(Stockfish Livorno-style)

Ingredients
500 g stockfish that has been soaked to remove the salt
400 g puréed tomatoes
1 onion
2 cloves of garlic
1 tablespoon chopped parsley
1 cup flour
e.v. olive oil

Remove the bones from the stockfish, cut it into pieces and dry with a cloth.

Peel and finely chop the onion with 1 clove of garlic, then sauté the chopped vegetables in a little oil. As soon as the onion begins to turn translucent, add the puréed tomatoes. Cook slowly over moderate heat for about 20 minutes, stirring constantly with a wooden spoon.

Heat a generous quantity of oil in a frying pan together with the remaining garlic. Lightly flour the pieces of stockfish and fry in the oil as soon as the gar-

POLENTA

Ingredients
300 g cornmeal
1 l of water
salt

Bring the water to a boil and sprinkle the cornmeal into it (it can be either fine or coarse-grained, as preferred). Stir constantly with a wooden spoon to keep lumps from forming.

For best results, cook at least 40-50 minutes. The polenta is done when it begins to detach from the sides of the pot.

lic has browned slightly. Drain the pieces of fish on paper towels and arrange on a preheated serving dish. Cover with the tomato sauce and sprinkle with the freshly chopped parsley.

Recommended wine
*Vernaccia
di San Gimignano*

Fishermen's delight

A dish characteristic of Lake Chiusi, sarcastically 'Porsenna's piss-hole', by the Lake Trasimeno dwellers, 'brustico' was traditionally prepared by fishermen over a reed-burning fire lit on the shore of the lake.

In the past, Lake Chiusi abounded in fish, and it was not a rare occurrence to witness this 'ritual' (today it's waters, like those of many other lakes in Italy, are sadly impoverished).

The traditional procedure was this: a fire was lit and, before the reeds had burned down entirely, the whole fish (with the interior) were placed on a grid over the fire.

In a few minutes a brown crust formed on the outside, while the meat inside cooked in its own juices.

When the fish were done the fishermen took them off the fire, scraped away the blackened skin and removed the bones and the interior.

The fish filets were then dressed with olive oil and seasoned with salt and pepper.

Brustico
(Barbecued fish)

A domesticated version of this recipe calls for thoroughly cleaning the fish, removing the entrails and washing them. Then build a fire and broil the fish over it, traditionally speared on a stick of laurel wood, until it is slightly burned on the outside. Remove the fish from the fire, detach the burned skin and place them on a serving dish.

Season with salt and pepper, crushed garlic, sage, rosemary and calamint, then dribble with olive oil.

Ingredients
800 g of mixed freshwater fish (pike, tench, eel or perch)
1 sprig of rosemary
a few sage leaves
calamint
garlic
e.v. olive oil

Recommended wine
Bianco di Pitigliano

Cacciucco alla livornese
(Livorno fish soup)

Ingredients

550 g cuttlefish, tattler, octupus
350 g soup fish (scorpion-fish, angler, swallow fish)
300 g mixed shellfish (clams, mussels)
200 g smooth hound
200 g scampi and crayfish
350 g peeled tomatoes
2 dl e.v. olive oil
2 onions
3 cloves of garlic
1 stalk of celery
1 carrot
3 sage leaves
1 bay leaf
hot red pepper
1 glass of dry white wine
4 slices of country-style bread

First clean the fish, removing the heads but retaining them. Remove the shells from the scampi and crayfish. Rid the shellfish of their impurities (when necessary). Remove the eyes and beaks from the cuttlefish, tattler and octupus and cut them in big pieces. Put a little water in a casserole. Add the carrot, stalk of celery, sage leaf, bay leaf and a clove of garlic and cook the fish heads in it. Strain the fish stock and set it aside. Chop the onion with the rest of the herbs and sauté in a large pot. When the onion is tender, add the cuttlefish, tattler and octupus. When the juices have reduced, add the wine. Once the wine has evaporated, add the chopped tomatoes and leave to cook for about 20 minutes. Then start to add the soup fish and the smooth hound. Add the stock made with the fish heads, taste for salt and cook until the cuttlefish, tattler and octupus become tender. At this point add the shellfish, scampi and crayfish. When the shells of the clams and mussels have opened wide, the cacciucco is ready. Arrange the toasted bread in individual bowls and cover with the soup.

Recommended wine
Val di Cornia rosso

Cacciucco

This recipe, typical of Livorno, has undergone numerous changes over the centuries. Originating in fact as soup to nourish seamen during navigation, it then fell prey to land-based cooks, who have variously interpreted it. "Cacciucco" belongs, however, to the vast family of fish soups that are found in every coastal regional. We need only think of the French "bouillabaisse" and all of the recipes that recur, under different names, along the coastline of Italy. The distinctive trait of Livornese "cacciucco" is, however, the use of hot red pepper.

Canocchie alla viareggina
(Squill-fish Viareggio-style)

Ingredients

2 kg squill-fish
2 cloves of garlic
1 piece of ginger
1 cup tomato sauce
e.v. olive oil
slices of country-style bread

Wash and dry the squill-fish carefully, then sauté in a pan with a little oil and with the peeled crushed garlic. Add the tomato sauce [see basic recipe, p. 45], the piece of ginger and, if necessary, a little water. Season with salt and pepper and cook over moderate heat for about 30 minutes

Recommended wine
Bolgheri bianco

Serve the fish on slices of toasted bread, basting with their cooking juices.

Luccio ripieno
(Stuffed pike)

Ingredients

1 pike, about 1 kg
1 onion
1 carrot
1 stalk of celery
100 g mixed bacon
fat and cured ham
1 clove of garlic
2 fresh sausages
1 glass white wine (or red)
1/2 cup e.v. olive oil

Clean and scale the pike, remove entrails and fins, wash and dry.

Prepare finely chopped vegetables with 1/2 onion, the carrot, celery, bacon fat and ham, salt and pepper, and use as stuffing to fill the fish, then close it with sewing thread or a skewer to keep the filling in. Chop the remaining onion, garlic and crumbled sausages together, mixing well. Place half of the mixture in a pan, preferably earthenware, with the oil.

Sauté gently, then place the pike on top of it, cover with the remaining half of the mixture, then add the white (or red) wine and cook for at least 1 hour. If the fish starts to dry out, add a little stock and baste frequently with its own juice.

Recommended wine
Bianco di Pitigliano

Bring the fish to the table in its own dish and serve very hot.

62

Palombo alla livornese
(Smooth dogfish Livorno-style)

Ingredients
4 slices of smooth dogfish
4 ripe but firm tomatoes
1 onion
1 carrot
1 glass red wine
1 cup of flour
e.v. olive oil

Prepare a mixture of finely chopped onion and carrot, and sauté gently in a few tablespoons of oil. When the vegetables have softened, add the lightly floured slices of fish and brown on both sides. Season with salt and pepper, and sprinkle with the red wine. Let the wine evaporate almost entirely, then add the peeled seed-free tomatoes cut into small pieces (after having plunged them in boiling water to loosen the skins). Cook over moderate heat, adding a little hot water if the fish tends to dry out.

This recipe can also be used with sliced swordfish in place of dogfish.

Recommended wine
Val di Cornia rosato

Tegamaccio
(Fish hotch-potch)

Ingredients
1 kg of mixed fish, pike,
  tench and eel
1 onion
2 cloves of garlic
1 glass of red wine (scant)
200 g fresh peeled tomatoes
  (or 80 g tomato preserves)
2-3 basil leaves
2 hot red peppers
4 slices country-style bread
e.v. olive oil

Fish hotch-potch is the most widely known speciality of the area round Lake Chiusi. It is a sort of freshwater fish soup, which should be prepared using at least two different types of fish. Its taste is further enhanced if it contains an abundant presence of eel.

After cleaning the fish and removing the entrails, wash it and cut it into pieces. Peel the onion and a clove of garlic, finely chop and sauté with a little oil in an earthenware pot, over moderate heat. Place the fish pieces in the browned vegetables and gently brown for a few minutes, then add the wine and allow to evaporate. Add salt and the hot red pepper. After a few minutes, add the basil leaves and the tomatoes passed through the vegetable mill (or tomato preserves diluted with a little hot water). Bring to the boil and simmer for about 2 hours, so that the sauce reduces, then remove from heat. Take out the large fish bones, remove all flesh from the heads and return the body and flesh to the pan. Meanwhile, toast the slices of bread in the oven, rub them with the remaining clove of garlic and place them in the pot to soak up the sauce. Serve immediately in the same pot, or, if you prefer, in individual bowls, placing a slice of toasted bread on the bottom of each bowl.

Recommended wine
Bolgheri rosato

Triglie alla livornese ▶▶
(Mullet Livorno-style)

Ingredients
8 fairly large mullet
500 g puréed tomatoes
1/2 onion
2 cloves of garlic
1/2 bay leaf
1 tablespoon chopped parsley
1 sprig of thyme
1/2 cup flour
e.v. olive oil

Prepare a very finely chopped mix of peeled onion and garlic together with the crushed chopped thyme. Then gently brown the vegetables in oil until the onion is translucent. Add the puréed tomatoes and cook over moderate heat for about 20 minutes, stirring occasionally with a wooden spoon.

Meanwhile clean the fish, then wash, dry and coat them in flour. Brown them lightly in a frying pan with a little oil, flavoured with the remaining peeled crushed clove of garlic.

Recommended wine
Montescudaio bianco
Bolgheri bianco

When the fish are well browned, drain them and place them in the pan with the tomato sauce. Add pepper and cook for another 10 minutes, occasionally turning the fish gently in the pan without breaking them. Serve garnished with finely chopped parsley.

# Meat

Agnello alle olive
(Lamb with olives)

Ingredients
1 kg lamb
250 g puréed tomatoes
150 g pitted black olives
4 cloves of garlic
1 glass of dry white wine
1 lemon
1 sprig of rosemary
1 tablespoon of vinegar
1 cup of stock
e.v. olive oil

V. Oct' 11. Main
Am good/easy

Different parts of lamb can be used for this dish, such as pieces of shoulder, neck, ribs, breast, etc.

Wash and dry the pieces of meat before gently sautéing in a little oil and vinegar to get rid of some of the fat.

Drain and transfer to a large pan in which you have previously sautéed the garlic and rosemary in a little oil. Season with salt and pepper and add the wine. When it has evaporated, remove the meat from the pan, keeping it warm. Add the puréed tomato and chopped olives.

Cook for a few moments and then add the pieces of lamb. Cook over low heat for about 1 hour, adding a little stock if the sauce starts to dry up. Serve boiling hot, preferably with slices of toasted polenta [see basic recipe, p. 58].

Recommended wine
Chianti Colli Senesi

Agnello arrosto
(Roast lamb)

Ingredients
1 leg of lamb (about 1 kg)
2 sprigs of rosemary
3 cloves of garlic
3 tablespoons of vinegar
1 glass of e.v. olive oil
whole black pepper

Mix the oil and vinegar. Chop the garlic and rosemary and add to the vinegar and oil, together with a pinch of salt and freshly ground pepper.

Wash and dry the meat. Then marinate in the vinegar and oil emulsion for about 2 hours, turning frequently.

When the lamb has absorbed all the flavours, cook in a preheated oven (200 °C), basting with the marinade.

When the lamb is half done, peeled and diced potatoes may be added to cook in the meat juices, as a magnificent accompaniment to the roast.

Recommended wine
Montescudaio rosso
Chianti Colli Aretini

Chianti, the Tuscan jewel

Chianti is probably the world's most famous Italian wine.

Distinguished by its typical ruby-red colour with garnet reflections that become deeper as it ages, an intense bouquet, with a delicate hint of violets, a balanced taste, dry, savoury, very slightly tannic, which become velvet with age, it is produced in a vast area of Tuscany spreading over the provinces of Arezzo, Florence, Pisa, Pistoia, and Siena, for which its name is now accompanied by a certified indication of geographic zone of production.

Thus we find Chianti Colli Aretini, Chianti Colli Senesi, Chianti Colli Fiorentini, Chianti Rufina, Chianti Colline Pisane, and Chianti di Montalbano.

The denomination "Classico" is reserved to wine made in the oldest production zone, which includes several communes situated in the provinces of Florence and Siena.

In general, Chianti has an alcohol content of 11.5°, which reaches 12° in the case of Chianti Classico.

The required ageing time is 4 months for Chianti and 7 months for Chianti Classico, Chianti Colli Fiorentini and Chianti Rufina.

The denomination "Riserva" can be used for wines that have been aged at least 3 years and have an alcohol content of 12°, which rises to 12.5° in the case of Chianti Classico.

It is a wine that should be uncorked an hour before serving and should be served at a temperature of 18-20 °C, with roasts, red meat, chicken, game and dry cheeses.

Anatra in porchetta
(Duck with pork stuffing)

Ingredients

1 duck (1.2 kg)
200 g sausage
100 g thick-cut Parma ham
6 thin slices of bacon fat
1 clove of garlic
2-3 bay leaves
1 sprig of rosemary
1 pinch of fennel seeds
1 glass of red wine
e.v. olive oil

(handwritten note)

Recommended wine
Carmignano rosso

Singe the duck and clean it, then wash and dry it. Dice the ham and mix with the crumbled sausage. Add the fennel seeds, chopped garlic and rosemary and a pinch of salt and pepper. Stuff the duck with this mixture. Then wrap it in the slices of bacon-fat and tie with kitchen twine. Slip the bay leaves in under the twine. Lightly season with salt and pepper. Place the duck in an oiled roasting pan and bake in a moderate oven (180°) for about 2 hours. When nearly done, sprinkle with the red wine. When the duck is ready, untie it and cut it in pieces, without separating the stuffing from the meat.

Arista (Roast saddle of pork) ▶▶

Ingredients

1 kg boned saddle of pork
2 cloves of garlic
a few sprigs of rosemary
e.v. olive oil
whole black pepper

Recommended wine
*Nobile
di Montepulciano*

Peel and chop the garlic. Mix it with salt and abundant freshly ground pepper. Then make incisions in the meat and stuff with the garlic mixture. Tie it with kitchen twine. Slip the rosemary, cut into short pieces, under the twine. Season the roast lightly with salt and pepper. Place it in a roasting tin well greased with olive oil and cook in a moderate oven (170-180 °C) for about 1 hour. When it is nearly done, turn up the oven to brown the roast well. Remove from the oven, untie and let the roast cool a little before slicing it. Place the slices on a serving dish and bast them with the cooking juices. In general, it is better to use a rather large piece of meat for this recipe. However, roast saddle of pork keeps very well in the fridge for a few days.

Arrosto di fegatelli
(Roast liver)

Ingredients
650 g pig's liver
with its "rete"(or netting)
1 slice of streaky bacon
1 handful of fennel seeds
2 bay leaves
1/2 glass red wine
2 tablespoons of wine vinegar
4 tablespoons of e.v. olive oil

Cut the liver into pieces of about 50 g each. Wrap each of them in a piece of netting, season with salt, pepper and fennel seeds, and fix the netting with toothpicks. Put the pieces of liver in a pan with the oil, the roughly chopped bacon, and the bay leaves. Cook over a fairly fast flame, stirring occasionally with a wooden spoon, and ladling the cooking fat over them. When they are nearly done, add the wine and vinegar and let evaporate. Serve piping hot. If preferred, the liver can also be cooked on a spit, alternating pieces of liver with cubes of bacon and bread.

Recommended wine
Chianti Classico
Nobile
di Montepulciano

Braciole del vinaio
(Veal chops in wine)

Ingredients
4 veal chops
40 g butter
1 glass of vinsanto (scant)
150 g fresh cep mushrooms
4 slices of sandwich bread
1/2 glass of milk
1 cup of flour
50 g grated parmesan
1 clove of garlic
4 tablespoons of e.v. olive oil
white pepper

Beat the steaks flat on a wooden cutting board with a meat hammer. Then clean the mushrooms, carefully removing earth and dirt. Wash them quickly under running water and dry them. Slice them and cook in a pan in which you have heated a little oil with the chopped garlic. Cook over a fairly high flame until the liquid evaporates, then lower the heat. When the mushrooms are done, set them aside.

Pour the milk in a bowl and rapidly dip the slices of bread in it. Then coat them with the flour and the parmesan. Melt a little butter in a frying pan and brown the slices of bread, then drain and set aside. Lightly coat the veal chops in the flour and cook in a pan with sizzling butter. Season with salt and pepper. Sprinkle with the wine and cook until it evaporates.

Place the slices of fried bread on a serving dish.

On top of each, put a veal chop covered with a table-spoon of mushrooms. Pour the cooking juices over them.

Recommended wine
Bianco di Pitigliano

Braciole in salsa rossa
(Veal chops in red sauce)

Ingredients
4 veal chops
300 g canned tomato pulp
1 egg
1 clove of garlic
1 bunch of fresh parsley
1 piece of ginger
3/4 cup of breadcrumbs
e.v. olive oil

Beat the eggs with a little salt and immerse the veal chops in them.

Chop the garlic, parsley and ginger and sauté in a little oil in a frying pan. Add the tomatoes, a little water and a pinch of salt and cook over moderate gentle heat with the lid on.

Remove the chops from the beaten eggs and coat them with the breadcrumbs. Fry them in a frying pan with abundant oil.

When done, drain them well and place them in the pan containing the tomato sauce. Turn them well to absorb the flavour, then serve.

Recommended wine
Montescudaio rosso

The "rete"

The "rete", also called "ratta" in Tuscany, is the fatty membrane that covers the intestinal tissue in the pig.

Thanks to its relative elasticity, it is used to wrap pieces of liver or other meat, to keep them compact during cooking. Furthermore, meat cooked in this netting is improved by the melting fat, which confers on it flavour and tenderness.

Butchers usually add the netting free of charge when pig's liver is purchased. In modern supermarkets it is often packaged together with the liver.

Buglione di agnello
(Lamb stew)

Ingredients

800 g lamb
2 medium-sized onions
2 cloves of garlic
1 hot red pepper
2 slices of streaky bacon
200 g peeled tomatoes
1 carrot
1 l of red wine
1/2 glass wine vinegar
2 beet leaves
1 sprig of sage
1 sprig of rosemary
1 stalk of celery
3-4 basil leaves
1 sprig of calamint
4 slices of country-style bread
1 cup of stock
e.v. olive oil

Cut the lamb into small pieces and marinate for a few hours, or better overnight, in red wine with a little vinegar and water, sage, rosemary, celery and basil.

After marinating, drain the pieces of lamb. Dry them with a clean cloth and place them in a pan over very gentle heat to remove any excess liquid.

Meanwhile, peel and chop 1 onion together with 1 clove of garlic and the hot red pepper.

Heat a little oil in a pan, preferably an earthenware casserole.

Sauté the chopped vegetables in it, then add the chopped bacon and brown a few more minutes.

Drain the pieces of lamb well and then add to the sautéed mixture. Brown them, stirring frequently with a wooden spoon.

Add the red wine and let it evaporate. Cook for a few minutes, then add the well-crushed peeled tomatoes, the remaining onion and the carrot, cleaned and thinly sliced, and the washed, dried and well chopped beet leaves.

As the sauce thickens, add a little hot stock. Season with salt, pepper and the calamint and continue to cook gently. Toast the slices of bread in the oven. Spread them with the remaining clove of garlic finely chopped with a pinch of pepper.

Arrange in a large serving dish and cover first with the sauce and then with the lamb pieces.

Recommended wine
Montescudaio rosso

Serve after a few minutes when the bread has soaked up the sauce.

Cappone ripieno arrosto
(Roast stuffed capon)

The quantities given here are sufficient for 6-8 people. Singe the capon and wash it, first with water and then with red wine. Stuff it with the bacon fat, sausages, 2 cloves of garlic and sage. Tie it well and season with salt and pepper. Peel and cut the potatoes in chunks. Toast the bread slices, rubbing them with 1 clove of garlic and dribbling them with oil.

Place the capon in a roasting pan with the loin of pork, potatoes, toasted bread rubbed with garlic and bay leaves. Sprinkle with the wine and put it in the oven preheated to 200 °C. Turn the capon frequently as it cooks and baste it with the melted fat.

When done, after about 1 1/2 hours, sprinkle with cognac. When this has evaporated, cut the capon into pieces and serve.

Ingredients
1 capon (2.5 kg, already cleaned)
3 thick slices of bacon fat
3 pork sausages
3 cloves of garlic
1 sprig of sage
1 tablespoon of butter
8 pieces of loin of pork
about 1 kg of potatoes
8 rounds of country-style bread
2-3 bay leaves
1 l of red wine
1 small glass of cognac
e.v. olive oil
white pepper

Recommended wine
Chianti Riserva Colli Senesi

Coniglio ripieno di carciofi
(Rabbit stuffed with artichokes)

At least 12 hours before cooking it, clean the rabbit and wash it in water and vinegar. Dry it and bard the more fleshy parts with strips of bacon and sprigs of rosemary.

Then clean the artichokes and plunge them into water into which a lemon has been squeezed. Cut them into quarters and stuff the rabbit with the artichokes, chopped garlic, tarragon and a little oil. Sew the opening with a needle and kitchen string so the stuffing

Ingredients
1 kg rabbit
4 artichokes
1 clove of garlic
80 g streaky bacon
1/2 lemon
1 sprig of rosemary
1 pinch of tarragon
1 l of white wine vinegar
e.v. olive oil

73

does not come out during cooking. Place the rabbit in a narrow pan and cover it almost entirely with the white wine. Cook it in the oven at moderate temperature (170-180 °C) until some of the wine has evaporated, leaving a rather thick liquid. At this point, increase the oven temperature to 200 °C, baste the rabbit with its juices, season with salt and pepper and continue cooking until it is pale brown in colour.

Recommended wine
Pomino rosso

Remove from the oven, cut away the string, cut into pieces and serve steaming hot.

Cibreo ▶▶
(Giblet fricassee)

Ingredients
400 g assorted chicken livers, combs and testicles
50 g butter
1/2 l of stock
1 tablespoon of flour
4 egg yolks
1 lemon

Clean the livers, removing the part attached to the bile. Clean the combs and blanch them for a few moments in boiling water with the livers. Then leave to drain. Wash the testicles too, plunging them in very hot water and, if necessary, removing bits of skin sticking to them. Skin the combs and cut them into pieces.

Chop the livers separately. In pan, preferably earthenware, heat the butter, add the combs and cook for 30 minutes, adding a little stock. Then add the livers and testicles. Season with salt and pepper and continue to cook. In the meantime, beat the egg yolks. Incorporate the lemon juice and the flour. Then gradually add 1 ladleful of boiling stock, stirring vigorously to keep the egg from cooking. Pour this mixture into the pot containing the giblets, stir and cook for a few minutes. Serve piping hot.

Recommended wine
Morellino di Scansano

Cinghiale in agrodolce
(Sweet and sour wild boar)

Ingredients

800 g boned shoulder
of wild boar
1 small onion
40 g streaky bacon
40 g butter
1 tablespoon of flour
40 g sugar
2 cloves of garlic
1/2 glass of vinegar
1 cup of stock
1 bay leaf
40 g bitter chocolate
30 g sultanas
30 g pine nuts
20 g candied citron
and orange
2 dried plums
4 cherries preserved in alcohol
MARINADE:
1 medium-sized onion
1 carrot
1 stalk of celery
1 clove of garlic
1 bunch of parsley
a few sprigs of thyme
a few bay leaves
a few cloves
1 l of dry white wine
1 glass of red wine vinegar
a few spice cloves
e.v. olive oil
whole black pepper
GARNISHING:
cherries preserved in alcohol

Start to marinate the wild boar meat 3 days before cooking.

Prepare the marinade by browning the finely chopped onion, carrot, celery, garlic, parsley, thyme and the bay leaves in an earthenware pot.

When they are golden brown, add the vinegar and 3-4 glasses of dry white wine, a few spice cloves and some peppercorns. Boil for a few minutes, then let cool.

Meanwhile tie the shoulder of wild boar as if preparing a roast, place it in a basin and pour over it the cooled marinade. If the meat is not entirely covered, add additional white wine. Cover and leave to marinate in the fridge for 3 days.

After this time, drain the meat (reserving the marinade), dry with a clean kitchen cloth and season with salt, pepper and a finely chopped clove of garlic. Then chop the streaky bacon with the remaining onion and brown in a little oil in a large pan.

Add the joint of wild boar. Brown evenly, then add the marinade, a little at a time. If the liquid is insufficient, add a little meat stock and more white wine. Simmer for 2 hours over low heat.

Then remove the meat from the cooking juices and set it aside. Strain the juices, add the butter, which has been cut into the flour, and mix, carefully smoothing out any lumps.

Prepare the sweet-and-sour sauce. Heat the sugar in an earthenware pot together with a clove of crushed garlic, a chopped bay leaf and the vinegar. Mix, and when the sugar has dissolved, add the grated bitter chocolate. When the chocolate has melted, add the chopped pine nuts, the washed, soaked and drained sultanas, the diced candied citron and orange, the plums and the alcohol-preserved cherries, chopped after removing the pips.

Add to the mixture the sauce prepared as described above and mix well.

Cut the wild boar in pieces, place in a pyrex dish, warm briefly over moderate heat and pour on the sweet-and-sour sauce.

Serve piping hot at table, garnished with some of the alcohol-preserved cherries.

Recommended wine
Nobile di Montepulciano

Cinghiale stufato
(Wild boar stew)

The day before cooking, pour the red wine into a basin and add the cleaned and sliced carrot, onion and celery, a peeled crushed clove of garlic, the spice clove, bay leaf and cinnamon.

Place the wild boar sirloin in this marinade and leave to marinate for 24 hours in a cool spot.

After this time, drain the meat and cut in pieces.

Peel the remaining clove of garlic, slice it and lightly brown it with a little oil in a pan, preferably earthenware. Add the lightly floured wild boar.

Season with salt, pepper and rosemary and brown well. Then add the peeled tomatoes and begin to pour

Ingredients
800 g wild boar sirloin
2 cloves of garlic
1 onion
1 carrot
1 stalk of celery
1 spice clove
1 pinch of cinnamon
1/2 cup flour
1 bay leaf
1 sprig of rosemary
1 l of red wine
80 g of fresh tomatoes
e.v. olive oil

in the marinade. Cover with a lid and simmer at moderate heat for about 2 hours (or until the meat is tender), stirring occasionally and adding more of the marinade if it is too dry.

Serve piping hot.

Recommended wine
*Morellino
di Scansano*

Morellino di Scansano

Ruby-red in colour, with a winey bouquet and dry flavour, Morellino di Scansano reaches an alcohol content of 11.5°.

When it is aged at least 2 years and has an alcohol content of 12°, it is qualified as "Riserva".

The production zone is found in the Province of Grosseto. The wine is produced from a minimum 85% of Sangiovese grapes, with the rest consisting of Canaiolo, Malvasia del Chianti, and other grapes.

It is best served at the temperature of 18 °C, as accompaniment to chicken and roasts.

Coda di manzo al pomodoro
(Oxtails in tomato sauce)

Ingredients
2 oxtails
500 g bottled tomato pulp
3 carrots
1 onion
1 stalk of celery
1 clove of garlic
a few leaves of sage
a few leaves of basil
1 sprig of rosemary
1 bunch of parsley
1 cup of stock
e.v. olive oil

Finely chop the fresh sage, rosemary, garlic, basil and parsley. In a large pan, sauté this mixture in a little oil until golden and then add the oxtails, cut in pieces.

Stir and brown the meat, then add the coarsely chopped carrots, celery and onion. Season with salt and pepper.

Add the tomato pulp and a little stock. Cover and cook for at least 2 hours over gentle heat.

Recommended wine
Montescudaio rosso

The oxtails are cooked when the meat comes away from the bone easily.

Faraona alla creta
(Guinea-fowl baked in a clay mould)

This fascinating recipe, in which the guinea-fowl is baked in a clay mould, can also be used for other birds: pheasant, pigeon or chicken.

First clean, wash and dry the guinea-fowl. Season the body cavity with salt, pepper, rosemary, sage and juniper berries. Bard it with slices of bacon. Then wrap it in well-greased oily paper. Next, encase it in a sheet of dampened yellow oven paper. Wet the clay (the best kind is the grey clay used to make terracotta tiles) and flatten it with your hands.

Place the bird in the middle and wrap the clay around it, moulding it into the shape of the bird. Seal it hermetically. Then place it in the oven at 180 °C and bake for 3 hours until the clay has dried and a few cracks start to appear. Break the mould in front of your guests using a small hammer. Take care to remove all the clay fragments and serve.

Ingredients
1 guinea-fowl (about 1.5 kg)
 already hung
4 slices of fatty bacon
1 sprig of sage
1 sprig of rosemary
4 juniper berries
4 tablespoons of e.v. olive oil

Recommended wine
*Brunello
di Montalcino*

Faraona nel cartoccio
(Guinea-fowl in foil)

Singe the bird and remove the entrails. Wash, dry and then stuff the bird with garlic, a few leaves of sage, salt and pepper. Season with salt on the outside. Cover it with slices of bacon, inserting several leaves of sage. Then wrap the bird in pig's abdomen netting and plunge into boiling water for 2-3 minutes. Drain and dry with a cloth. At this point, brush a sheet of oilpaper with oil

Ingredients
1 guinea-fowl (about 1.5 kg)
 already hung
100 g sliced bacon
1 piece of pig's abdomen
 netting
1 sprig of sage
2 cloves of garlic
3 tablespoons of e.v. olive oil

Recommended wine
Chianti Colline Pisane

and wrap it round the guinea-fowl. Then place it in a roasting pan and put it in the oven at 180 °C for about 1 hour. Make sure that the paper does not burn. Serve the guinea-fowl and carve it at the table.

Fagiano tartufato
(Truffled pheasant)

Ingredients
1 pheasant (about 1.2 kg) already hung
150 g cured ham with its fat in a single slice
150 g bacon
150 g black truffles
1/2 glass cognac
1 glass dry white wine
1 sprig sage
250 ml cream
e.v. olive oil

The day before cooking the pheasant, prepare the stuffing. Clean the truffles thoroughly, chop them (leaving some flakes for decoration), mix them with the chopped ham and amalgamate with a little cognac. Stuff the pheasant with this mixture and place it in the refrigerator for a few hours to absorb the fragrance of the truffles. Prior to cooking, wrap the bird in the slices of bacon, inserting a few leaves of sage, and tie it well with kitchen twine. Season with salt and pepper and place in a pan, preferably earthenware, with a little oil. Cover and brown over direct heat for a few minutes, then place the pan, still covered, in the oven at 200 °C. Cook for about 20 minutes, then remove the cover and moisten the bird with the white wine. Let the wine evaporate, then baste with the melted fat and continue cooking at a lower temperature. When the pheasant is done, remove it from oven, cut it in pieces and reserve the stuffing. Add the rest of the cognac to the gravy that is left in the pan, skim off the excess fat, then add the pheasant stuffing and the cream and boil for a few minutes.

Arrange the pieces of pheasant in a pyrex dish, pour over them the gravy mixed with the stuffing, and garnish with truffle flakes.

Recommended wine
Brunello di Montalcino

Fiorentina
(Florentine steak)

Ingredients

2 sirloin beef steaks
e.v. olive oil

A good Florentine steak requires top quality meat which has been well aged. It should be about 2.5 cm thick, not having been beaten and weigh about 500 g.

First prepare the charcoal fire. Heat the grill before placing the steaks on top.

When one side is cooked, turn them over and season the grilled side with salt and pepper. Then turn them again to dissolve the salt so that it is evenly distributed and any excess runs off. Remove the steaks from the grill when they are well browned on the outside but still tender and rare on the inside. Arrange them on a hot dish, accompanied by fresh olive oil, if desired.

Recommended wine

Chianti Colli Fiorentini

Francesina
(French stew)

Ingredients

500 g boiled meat
300 g white onions
300 g peeled tomatoes
100 g leeks
1 glass of red wine
1 clove of garlic
1 cup of stock
powdered hot red pepper
e.v. olive oil

This recipe uses cheaper cuts of meat which are usually used for making stock.

Clean and slice fine the onion and leek (only the white part) and gently sauté in an earthenware pot together with the peeled and crushed garlic. When they are tender, add the diced boiled meat, a pinch of hot red pepper, salt, freshly ground black pepper and the red wine, stirring gently.

When the wine has evaporated, add the chopped tomatoes. Simmer for 40 minutes, adding a little meat stock if it starts to dry. Serve with slices of toasted polenta [see basic recipe, p. 58] if you wish.

Recommended wine

Montescudaio rosso

Galletto con funghi
(Chicken with mushrooms)

Ingredients

1 cockerel (about 1 kg)
350 g cep mushrooms
1 medium-sized onion
2 glasses of dry white wine
1 cup of stock
1 sprig of calamint
1 small glass of grappa
e.v. olive oil

Singe the bird and remove the entrails. Wash, dry and cut into small pieces. Clean the mushrooms, scraping the stalks with a knife. Wipe with a damp cloth, slice and set aside.

Peel the onion, cut into rounds and brown lightly in a little oil in a pot, preferably earthenware. Then add the pieces of chicken.

Brown carefully and then season with salt and pepper. Add nearly all the white wine and cook until it evaporates.

Then add the mushrooms with a little meat stock and cook for 30 minutes at moderate heat. Lastly, add the remaining wine and a few calamint leaves; taste for salt and pepper.

Recommended wine
*Rosato
di Carmignano*

Before serving, sprinkle with the grappa. Serve piping hot.

Gallinella alle olive
(Young hen with olives)

Ingredients

1 young hen (about 1.2 kg)
1 medium-sized onion
1 carrot
1 stalk of celery
1 glass of red wine
1 cup of stock
200 g green olives in brine
200 g spring onions
1/2 glass of e.v. olive oil

Clean the hen, removing the entrails. Wash, dry and cut into 8 pieces. Heat the oil in an earthenware pot. Peel the onion, clean and wash the carrot and the celery. Chop the vegetables, add to the oil and sauté over gentle heat.

Add the pieces of hen, browning on all sides, then sprinkle with the red wine. If necessary, add a ladleful of meat stock. Season with salt and pepper and cook over medium heat.

Meanwhile peel and blanch the spring onions in boiling water. Then drain and set aside. When the hen is done, remove it from the pan. Rub the juices and vegetables through a sieve and return to the pan, adding the pieces of hen.

Then wash the olives and blanch the spring onions in boiling water. Add them to the sauce. If necessary, add a little stock. Cook until the sauce has thickened. Serve hot.

Recommended wine
Chianti Classico

Insalata di trippa
(Tripe salad)

Ingredients
600 g pre-cooked tripe
200 g dried "cannellini" beans
200 g spring onions
200 g potatoes
1 celery heart
whole white pepper
baking soda

Tripe is a great Tuscan passion and there are a thousand different, original ways of preparing it. A connoisseur's delight, this recipe can be served cold as a substantial snack or as a summer dish.

The day before cooking, put the beans to soak overnight. The next day, drain them and boil them with a pinch of baking soda. Boil the potatoes separately; drain and leave to cool.

Wash the tripe and cook it in boiling water for 10 minutes. Then cut it into strips.

Finely slice the onions and celery and dice the cooked, peeled potatoes (now cool). Add all the ingredients to the tripe and season with plenty of oil, salt, and freshly ground white pepper. Carefully stir and serve when fully cooled.

Recommended wine
Chianti Classico

Lepre in salmì
(Hare in salmì)

Ingredients

1 hare (about 2 kg)
1 l red wine
300 g of champignons
20 g bacon in a single slab
30 small onions
1 stick celery
1 carrot
1 onion
1 clove of garlic
a few sage leaves
1 sprig of rosemary
1 small glass of brandy
100 g butter
50 g flour
1 dl hare's blood
1 dl cream

The quantities given here are for 8 persons.

Clean the hare (reserving 1 dl of the blood) and cut it in pieces. In a bowl prepare the marinade with the wine, the cleaned and coarsely chopped celery, carrot, and onion, the crushed garlic and the sage and rosemary leaves. Place the pieces of hare in the marinade and leave them for 48 hours.

Then drain the meat, dry it and sauté in a casserole with a tablespoon of sizzling butter. When well browned, dredge with flour, flame with brandy, add the marinade and season with salt, then continue cooking at medium heat for about 2 hours.

Meanwhile, dice the bacon, blanch it and brown it in a frying pan. Clean the onions and sauté in a little butter. Clean the mushrooms and rinse briefly under running water, dry, slice and sauté in the remaining butter. Add the vegetables to the hare and cook for another 15 minutes.

Shortly before removing from the heat, add the cream mixed with the reserved hare's blood. Simmer for a few minutes and serve.

Recommended wine
Carmignano rosso

Lesso rifatto
(Twice-cooked boiled meat)

Ingredients

500 g leftover boiled meat
1 onion
300 g ripe tomatoes
a few leaves of fresh basil
4 tablespoons of e.v. olive oil

This recipe, also known as "stiracchio", does not require much effort or time.

Cut the boiled meat into slices. Wash the tomatoes,

remove their seeds and chop into tiny pieces. Peel and chop the onion and sauté in a little oil over medium heat. When lightly browned, add the meat, tomatoes, basil, salt and pepper. Cover and cook for about 10 minutes over low heat.

When done, arrange the slices of meat on a serving dish and pour the sauce over them.

Recommended wine
Parrina rosso

Ossibuchi alla fiorentina
(Shin of veal Florentine-style)

Peel the onion and garlic and chop together with a handful of fresh basil. In a frying pan, heat the butter and gently sauté the vegetables. Then add the shin of veal and brown slowly.

Sprinkle with the marsala. When it has evaporated, add the tomato pulp, stock, salt and pepper, then simmer gently.

The veal is done when the prongs of a fork sink into the meat easily, about 1 1/2 hours.

Ingredients
4 slices of shin of veal
600 g of canned tomato pulp
1 small onion
1 clove of garlic
1 bunch of basil
1 glass of marsala
1 cup of stock
30 g butter

Recommended wine
Chianti Colli Fiorentini

Brunello di Montalcino

Considered one of the greatest Italian wines, the world-famous Brunello di Montalcino was practically created in the second half of the 19th century by the skilled hand of Ferruccio Biondi-Santi, who began to make wine from a clone of Sangiovese, which was called Brunello.

A red wine of brilliant ruby colour tending toward garnet with ageing, it has a distinctive bouquet and a dry, robust, harmonious, warm taste. The production zone is the territory of Montalcino, an ancient town in the Province of Siena, dominated by the imposing bulk of its 14th-century castle.

Lombata di vitello al forno ▶▶
(Roasted veal sirloin)

Ingredients

1 kg loin of veal
50 g bacon
3 sage leaves
1 sprig of rosemary
1 clove of garlic
e.v. olive oil

Finely chop the sage, rosemary and garlic and spread on top of the slices of bacon on a working surface. Season the loin with salt and pepper, then place it on top of the bacon. Wrap the bacon round the loin and tie it firmly with kitchen string.

Lightly grease a roasting pan with oil. Put the loin in it and place in the oven at 250 °C.

After 20 minutes, lower the temperature to 140 °C and leave to cook for 1 hour more. At this point, turn the oven off but leave the roast inside for another 20 minutes so that the meat cooks inside but remains pink. Remove the outer covering, cut the roast into fairly thick slices and serve.

Recommended wine
Bianco Vergine
Valdichiana

Piccioni in arrosto morto
(Pigeons in a casserole)

Ingredients

4 young pigeons
1 onion
80 g bacon fat
1 clove of garlic
2 sausages
1 glass of red wine
1 cup of stock
e.v. olive oil

Flame the pigeons, clean and remove entrails; wash and dry the birds. Peel the onion and chop half of it together with the bacon fat, sausages, salt and pepper. Fill the gullet of each pigeon with the chopped mixture and then place the birds in a casserole, preferably earthenware, with a little oil and a finely chopped blend of the remaining garlic and onion. Cook over low heat adding a little stock now and then; when the pigeons are nearly done, add a little red wine and let it evaporate. Serve the pigeons piping hot.

Recommended wine
Brunello
di Montalcino

Piccioni ripieni
(Stuffed pigeons)

Ingredients

4 young pigeons
2 sausages
2 eggs
100 g of lean veal
soft bread from inside
2-3 rolls
40 g of grated parmesan
1 glass of milk
1 small onion
1 pinch of calamint
(or marjoram)
nutmeg
1 tablespoon of butter
1 cup of stock
e.v. olive oil

Flame the pigeons, then remove the entrails, setting them aside; wash the birds and dry with a cloth. Meanwhile soak the bread with milk in a basin.

Clean and wash the pigeon giblets, allow to drain and then chop them together with the sausage and lean veal.

Squeeze out the softened bread and add to the chopped ingredients, then work in the eggs, salt, pepper, a pinch of nutmeg and the grated parmesan.

Stuff the pigeons with this mixture. Season them with salt and pepper and arrange in a pan with the oil and butter, the peeled and chopped onion, a pinch of calamint (or marjoram).

Cover and cook over low heat for about 1 hour, stirring occasionally with a wooden spoon. If necessary, add a little meat stock.

Serve the pigeons piping hot.

Recommended wine
*Nobile
di Montepulciano*

Pollo al mattone
(Barbecued chicken)

Ingredients

1 young chicken (about 1 kg)
2 cloves of garlic
1 sprig of sage
powdered hot red pepper
e.v. olive oil
TO GARNISH:
1 lemon

Prepare the chicken for this dish the day before cooking. Clean, wash and dry the chicken. Cut it into 2 parts and flatten with a meat hammer. Put it in a bowl with plenty of oil, the peeled and sliced garlic and a few sage leaves. Marinate in the fridge overnight.

Next morning, remove the chicken from the fridge.

Place it skin side down on a grill (preferably over a wood or charcoal fire) and season well with salt, pepper and ground powdered hot red pepper. Place a brick on top and grill it, taking care that the fire is not too hot.

Then remove the brick, turn the chicken over, brush it with a little oil and cover it with the brick again. Bear in mind that all together it will take about 40 minutes to cook.

Serve with lemon quarters.

Recommended wine
Bolgheri rosato

Pollo all'arrabbiata
(Chicken 'in a hurry')

The term "all'arrabbiata" is used to indicate many different things in cooking. In this case, it refers to the speed at which the dish is prepared.

First of all, singe the bird and remove the entrails. Then wash and dry it and cut into fairly small pieces.

Wash and dry the carrot and celery, then chop finely together with the onion and garlic and sauté in a pan, preferably earthenware, with a little oil.

After a few minutes add the chicken pieces lightly coated in flour. Brown gently. Then add the red wine and cook until it evaporates before adding the peeled, puréed tomatoes and the hot red pepper. Season with salt and pepper.

Cook over medium heat for about 1/2 hour. If the sauce is too dry, add a little hot meat stock. When done, sprinkle with finely chopped parsley and basil and serve piping hot.

Ingredients
1 young chicken (about 1 kg)
1 small onion
1 carrot
1 stalk of celery
2 cloves of garlic
1 glass of red wine
200 g fresh peeled tomatoes
1 hot red pepper
1 cup of stock
1 cup flour
1 bunch of parsley
3 basil leaves

Don't cook chicken too long! soggy! (handwritten note)

Recommended wine
Chianti Classico
Nobile
di Montepulciano

Pollo alla diavola
(Devilled chicken)

Ingredients

1 chicken (about 1.2 kg)
1 cup of e.v. olive oil
1 lemon
hot red pepper
TO GARNISH:
1 lemon

Clean the chicken and cut it in half. Then flatten it with a meat hammer on a wooden cutting board, taking care not to break the bones.

In a bowl, prepare a sauce by emulsifying the oil with the lemon juice, salt, pepper and a good pinch of hot red pepper. Marinate the chicken in this sauce for about 1/2 hour, turning it frequently.

Cook the chicken over a barbecue, or if this is not possible under the oven grill.

Recommended wine

*Nobile
di Montepulciano*

After about 40 minutes, serve the chicken garnished with slices of lemon and, if you like, with a side dish of salad greens.

Pollo in fricassea
(Chicken fricassee)

Ingredients

1 young chicken (about 1 kg)
1 medium-sized onion
1 carrot
1 stalk of celery
4 tablespoons e.v. olive oil
1 tablespoon butter
250 ml stock
1 bunch of parsley
1 tablespoon of flour
2 egg yolks
1 lemon

Wash the chicken, dry it and cut it into pieces. Clean, wash and dry the carrot, stalk of celery and parsley and tie them in a little bundle together with the sliced onion.

Heat the oil and butter in a pan, preferably earthenware. Add a tablespoon of flour and stir carefully with a wooden spoon. When the roux starts to brown, add a little meat stock and stir.

When it starts to boil, add the bundle of vegetables and cook over medium heat for a few minutes. Then add the chicken, salt and pepper. Cover and cook for about 1/2 hour, stirring occasionally. If the sauce becomes too dry, add a little more stock. Meanwhile beat the egg yolks in a bowl with the lemon juice. When the chicken is done, remove the bundle of vegetables. Take the pot off the heat and pour the egg yolk mixture onto the chicken, stirring vigorously to obtain a smooth sauce. Serve.

Recommended wine
Chianti Classico

Pollo fritto alla toscana
(Fried chicken Tuscan-style)

Ingredients
1 chicken (about 1.2 kg)
250 g l flour
5 eggs
e.v. olive oil

Carefully clean the chicken and remove the bones. Cut in pieces.

In a bow, beat the eggs with a pinch of salt and 1 tablespoon of oil. Then add the flour a little at a time, mixing continuously, to form a thick, smooth batter. Coat the chicken pieces in the batter and deep fry in hot oil. When browned, drain and dry on absorbent paper towels before placing on a serving dish.

This recipe can be prepared using chicken breasts alone.

Recommended wine
Chianti Classico

Polmoncino rifatto
(Twice-cooked lung)

Ingredients
600 g calf's lung
1/2 glass of wine vinegar
1 medium-sized onion
1 glass of red wine
1 cup of stock
200 g ripe tomatoes
1 bunch of parsley
1 hot red pepper
1/2 glass of e.v. olive oil

First rinse the calf's lung under running water, then cut it in cubes and put it to soak in water with a little wine vinegar for about 1 1/2 hours.

Meanwhile, peel and finely chop the onion and sauté it gently in a pan, preferably earthenware.

Drain and dry the lung. Add it to the sautéed onion

and brown, stirring frequently with a wooden spoon. Season with salt and pepper. Sprinkle with red wine. When it has evaporated, add the hot red pepper and puréed tomatoes (peeled after having been plunged briefly into boiling water to loosen the skins).

Cook over moderate heat, adding a little meat stock if it becomes too dry.

If you prefer, before adding the tomatoes, enrich the dish with a little chopped streaky bacon or some skinned and crumbled sausage.

Just before serving, sprinkle with a little chopped parsley.

Recommended wine
Morellino
di Scansano

Polpette di trippa
(Tripe balls)

Ingredients
400 g pre-cooked tripe
250 g puréed tomatoes
50 g cured ham
the soft inside of 2 bread rolls
30 g grated parmesan
2 eggs
1 bunch of parsley
1 onion
1 carrot
2 cloves of garlic
3 leaves of basil
1 cup of flour
2 tablespoons of milk
nutmeg
e.v. olive oil

Wash the tripe and blanch in boiling water. Grind it in a meat grinder together with the ham.

Put it in a bowl and add the bread softened in milk, squeezed dry and crumbled, the eggs, grated parmesan, chopped parsley and basil, salt, pepper and a pinch of nutmeg.

Stir carefully to incorporate all the ingredients, then mould the mixture into little balls. Lightly coat with flour and deep-fry in hot oil.

When the meatballs are done, dry them on paper towels. Then sauté the finely chopped garlic, carrot, and onion in a little oil in a wide pan. When the vegetables are soft, add the meatballs and the puréed tomatoes. Cover and cook gently for about 1 hour.

Recommended wine
Chianti Conti
Serristori

Polpettone
(Meat loaf)

Ingredients
300 g boiled beef
2 sausages
80 g soft bread
1/2 l of stock
2 eggs
1 tablespoon butter
40 g parmesan
3 tablespoons flour
nutmeg
2 tablespoons of e.v. olive oil

Even if it contains meat, meat loaf is traditionally considered an economical dish, being made of leftovers from boiled beef or stews.

First grind the meat in a food mill with the sausage and the soft bread, previously damped with stock and squeezed dry. Add the eggs, grated parmesan, salt, pepper, and a pinch of nutmeg and mix well. Shape into a long, rather thick meatloaf.

Peel and chop the onion. Sauté it gently in the oil and butter in a medium-sized ovenproof dish. Then add the meatloaf lightly coated with flour. Place the dish in an oven preheated to 160-170 °C and cook the meatloaf, occasionally adding hot meat stock. After about 30 minutes, remove the meat loaf from the oven. Leave it to cool well, slice it, arrange the slices on a serving dish and serve.

Recommended wine
Rosso Colline
Lucchesi

Rognoni in teglia
(Fried kidneys)

Ingredients
500 g calves' kidneys
1 bunch of parsley
1/2 cup breadcrumbs
whole black pepper
e.v. olive oil
TO GARNISH:
1 lemon

Wash and parboil the kidneys for about 20 minutes in lightly salted water.

Open them lengthwise and remove the gristly core. Sauté in a frying pan with a little oil.

When lightly browned, remove from the heat and season with salt, freshly ground pepper and finely chopped parsley.

Leave to rest for at least an hour, stirring frequently

so that the seasoning is evenly distributed. Remove the kidneys from the pan, and put the pan back on the fire. Coat the kidneys in breadcrumbs and put back in the pan to sauté in the cooking juices.

Serve the kidneys crisp and golden, garnished with lemon quarters.

Recommended wine
Morellino di Scansano

Scottiglia
(Meat stew)

Ingredients
1 kg of mixed meats
(guinea-fowl, chicken,
rabbit, pigeon, veal, pork)
1 onion
1 carrot
1 stalk of celery
500 g fresh tomatoes
2 cloves of garlic
1 hot red pepper
1 bunch of parsley
2 lemons
1 glass of red wine
250 ml of meat stock
6 slices of country-style bread
e.v. olive oil

First clean the fowls, wash, dry and and cut into pieces. Cut the lean pork and veal into pieces.

Peel 1 clove of garlic and the onion, clean and wash the celery, carrot and parsley. Chop them fine with the hot red pepper and sauté in a large pot, preferably earthenware, in 3-4 tablespoons of hot oil. When the vegetables are golden, add the meat and brown over a fairly fast flame, turning with a wooden spoon. Add the lemon juice, let it evaporate and add the red wine. Cook over moderate heat until the sauce has thickened considerably. Then add the tomatoes (peeled after having been briefly plunged in boiling water to loosen the skins) and a little stock.

Season with salt and continue to cook, stirring occasionally. When the stew is done, there should be quite a lot of thinnish sauce.

Toast the slices of bread in the oven and rub them with the remaining clove of garlic.

Place them in the soup bowls, cover with the pieces of meat and the sauce. Leave to rest for a few minutes and then serve.

Recommended wine
Chianti Classico

96

Spezzatino rifinito
(Veal stew)

Ingredients
600 g lean veal muscle
1 medium-sized onion
1 carrot
1 stalk of celery
1 clove of garlic
a few basil leaves
1 glass red wine
350 g ripe tomatoes
1 cup of stock
e.v. olive oil

Cut the muscle into 50 g pieces. Peel the onion and garlic. Clean and wash the carrot, stalk of celery and basil leaves. Chop together and sauté in a large pan with abundant oil over gentle heat, stirring with a wooden spoon. When lightly browned, add the meat and cook for about 10 minutes over a fairly fast flame, stirring often. Then sprinkle with the red wine and let it evaporate.

In the meantime, wash and peel the tomatoes and put them through a sieve. Add them to the stew and season with salt and pepper.

Cook for 2 1/2 hours over low heat, adding meat stock if the stew becomes too dry.

Serve with beans in tomato sauce ("fagioli all'uccelletto") [see recipe, p. 45] cooked separately and added to the stew at the last minute.

Recommended wine
*Nobile
di Montepulciano*

Tordi finti
(Stuffed veal rolls)

Ingredients
8 veal chops
8 slices of cured ham
  with its fat
8 leaves of sage
1 small onion
40 g bacon fat
1/2 glass of red wine
1 cup stock
e.v. olive oil

The name of the recipe means 'mock thrushes' and is also known as "uccelletti finti" ('mock birds') or "topini" ('little mice').

Beat the chops flat on a wooden cutting board, using a meat hammer, and lay them out on the counter. Then peel, slice and finely chop the onion with the bacon; season with salt and pepper. Put a slice of ham and a sage leaf on each veal chop, then spread with the chopped onion and bacon fat. Roll up each chop and fasten with a toothpick. Place the veal rolls in an oven-proof dish, dribble with oil and season with salt and pepper. Cook in a preheated oven at 220 °C for about 15 minutes, occasionally adding a little hot stock. Lastly, sprinkle with the wine and let it evaporate.

When the veal rolls are well browned, serve straight from the oven.

Recommended wine
Montecarlo rosso

Trippa alla fiorentina
(Tripe Florentine-style)

Ingredients
700 g pre-cooked tripe
400 g peeled tomatoes
50 g grated parmesan
2 onions
2 cloves of garlic
1 carrot
e.v. olive oil

Carefully wash the tripe and blanch it for 10 minutes in boiling water. Then rinse it in cold water, dry it and cut it into strips.

Clean and finely chop the onion, carrot and garlic and sauté in a frying pan with a little oil. When the onion is tender, add the tripe and after a few minutes the peeled and chopped tomato. Season with salt and pepper, cover and cook until, on tasting, the tripe melts in your mouth. If when the tripe is nearly done the sauce is too liquid, let it simmer without the lid until it thickens. Lastly, stir in the grated parmesan, mix well and serve.

Recommended wine
Chianti Colli
Fiorentini

Side dishes

Cappelle di porcini al gratin (Mushroom caps au gratin)

Ingredients
13 medium-sized cep mushrooms
1 onion
2 cloves of garlic
1 egg
50 g parmesan
100 g lean ground meat
soft inside of 1 bread roll
1 tablespoon chopped parsley
1/2 cup breadcrumbs
e.v. olive oil

Clean the mushrooms carefully. Reserve 1 of them, to be used for the stuffing. Detach the caps from the other 12 mushrooms and put them in a hot oven for 5 minutes to dry them a little. Meanwhile, chop the reserved mushroom together with all the stems. In a saucepan, heat a little oil and sauté peeled and finely sliced onion and garlic; as soon as they become translucent, add the ground meat. Stir and brown the meat for a few minutes before adding the chopped mushroom and parsley. Cook for another 5 minutes, then remove from the heat and incorporate the egg-yolk and the soft bread, which has been moistened in water, squeezed dry and crumbled. Mix vigorously to form a smooth paste, that will be used to fill the mushroom caps. Dust the stuffed mushrooms with breadcrumbs and place in a hot oven (200 °C) for about 20 minutes, to gratinate.

Cardi rifatti (Twice-cooked cardoons)

Ingredients
650 g of white cardoons
2 eggs
1 cup flour
1 lemon
200 g tomato sauce
e.v. olive oil

Clean and wash the cardoons carefully, eliminating the fuzz and filaments, then boil in water to which lemon juice has been added. Drain well.

Meanwhile, break the eggs and reserve the whites.

Flour the cardoons, dip them in the lightly beaten egg whites, and deep-fry them in hot oil. Drain them well on paper towels. In a separate pan, heat the tomato sauce [see basic recipe, p. 45], add the cardoons, season with salt and pepper and cook over low heat, and. The cardoons are done when they have almost completely absorbed the sauce. Serve piping hot.

Carciofi ripieni (Stuffed artichokes)

Ingredients
4 large artichokes (8 if small)
1 lemon
20 g dried mushrooms
80 g chicken livers
1 sausage
50 g streaky bacon
1/2 cup soft bread
1 bunch of parsley
1 egg
1 small onion
1/2 cup of stock
1 glass dry white wine
1 tablespoon butter
e.v. olive oil

Clean and wash the artichokes, remove the tough outer leaves, and place in a pot of boiling water soured with lemon juice. Blanch the artichokes briefly and drain as soon as the water comes back to the boil. Allow to cool. Meanwhile wash the dried mushrooms and soak them in a little warm water. Soak the bread in a little stock, then squeeze it dry.

When the artichokes have cooled, remove the stalk, scoop out their insides, and chop the insides together with the stalk in a bowl. Squeeze dry and chop the mushrooms.

Chop the chicken livers, crumble the sausage and the squeezed soft bread, and add these ingredients to the bowl containing the finely chopped onion, parsley and streaky bacon. Lastly, add the egg yolk, season with salt and pepper and mix well. Fill the artichokes with this mixture. Place them in a deep pan with abundant oil, flake them with butter and dust with white pepper.

Cover, and bake in a moderate oven for 30 minutes. Then sprinkle the artichokes with the white wine and continue to cook covered for another 1/2 hour.

Fagioli al fiasco
(Beans in a bottle)

Ingredients
350 g shelled "canellini" beans
2 cloves garlic
6 sage leaves
1/2 glass e.v. olive oil

This recipe is an ancient tradition that calls for time and patience. First, take a two-litre wide-neck glass flask, remove the straw casing and wash carefully. Fill it 2/3 full of beans, then add the oil and the coarsely chopped sage, crushed garlic and about 2 glasses of water. Stop up the bottle with the straw casing, or use tow, oakum or cotton, but without pressing down too hard, so that the steam can escape during the cooking process.

At this point the Tuscan farmers used to place the flask upright on the glowing embers covered with warm ashes, allowing the beans to cook for at least 5 hours or even overnight.

In the lack of a fireplace, you can place the flask in the oven at moderate heat, in a pyrex dish half filled with water. The beans are done when all the water in the flask has evaporated and the oil has been completely absorbed. Take the beans out of the bottle, add salt and lots of pepper and drench them with e.v. olive oil.

Fagioli all'uccelletto
(Beans in tomato sauce)

Ingredients
500 g shelled fresh "cannellini" beans
2 cloves of garlic
3-4 sage leaves
150 ml of puréed tomatoes
e.v. olive oil

Pour the beans into an earthenware pot and cover with cold, lightly salted water. Place the pot over heat, bring rapidly to the boil, cover and reduce heat to barely perceptible simmering for 1 hour, then drain.

In a saucepan, heat a little oil and sauté the garlic

and sage, then add the beans, still warm. Stir and cook for 5 minutes. Add the puréed tomatoes, salt and pepper and cook uncovered for about 15 minutes.

"Fagioli all'uccelletto" is a highly flexible recipe, since it can serve as side dish to a wide variety of main dishes, but can also be used as a main dish in its own right.

Funghi in fricassea
(Fricasseed mushrooms)

Ingredients
800 g cep mushrooms
1 onion
60 g butter
2 egg yolks
1 lemon
1 bunch of parsley

Using a sharp kitchen knife, delicately scrape the stem of each mushroom in order to remove the earthy part, then wipe clean with a damp cloth. Cut into fairly large pieces. Peel and chop the onion, then sauté it with the butter in a pan, preferably earthenware. Add the mushrooms and cook over low heat, mixing delicately. Season with salt and pepper and continue cooking (for about 20 minutes.) Remove from heat and add the egg yolks beaten together with the lemon juice. Stir well and serve at table garnished with a dusting of chopped parsley.

Melanzane rifatte in trippa
(Twice-cooked aubergines)

Ingredients
550 g aubergine, 2 eggs
tomato sauce
1 slice of streaky bacon
1 cup of flour
1/2 cup grated breadcrumbs
grated pecorino
1/2 glass vinegar
e.v. olive oil

Clean, peel and slice the aubergines, cut into wide slices and layer them in a sufficiently large colander. Sprinkle each layer with a pinch of salt, and spray with a little vinegar. Cover and weight down the cover;

leave to sweat and drain for at least 8 hours. Then wash and dry the aubergine slices.

In a bowl, beat the eggs with a pinch of salt. Dip the aubergine slices in the beaten eggs, then in flour mixed with breadcrumbs, and deep-fry in hot oil. Drain well and leave to dry on paper towels.

Meanwhile, finely chop the bacon, sauté it lightly and add the tomato sauce [see basic recipe, p. 45]. Continue cooking for a few minutes.

Place the aubergine slices in a shallow pan and pour the sauce over them. Put the pan in the oven at 170 °C to finish cooking. Serve piping hot, dusted with grated pecorino.

Stufato di fave
(Stewed broad beans)

Ingredients
2 kg of unshelled broad
beans
1 medium-sized onion
150 g ripe tomatoes
80 g cured ham with its fat
1 cup of stock
1 bunch of parsley
1-2 cloves of garlic
e.v. olive oil
slices of country-style bread

Shell the broad beans, wash under running water and drain.

Meanwhile peel and finely chop the onion together with the parsley and ham. Heat an abundant quantity of oil in a pan and add the chopped mixture; sauté over moderate heat, mixing with a wooden spoon. Add the broad beans, and stew over low heat, adding a little beef stock occasionally.

About 10 minutes before removing from heat, add the tomatoes, peeled (after having been briefly plunged in boiling water to loosen the skins) and put through a food mill. Return to heat and add salt and pepper to taste. Serve with slices of toasted bread rubbed with garlic.

Tortino di carciofi (Artichoke pie)

Ingredients

4 tender artichokes
6 eggs
40 g pecorino
1 lemon
1 bunch of parsley
e.v. olive oil

Clean the artichokes, removing the tough outer leaves and cut them into segments. Place them in a pot of water soured with lemon juice, and boil them. When done, drain and place in a bowl in which 4 eggs have been beaten with half of the grated pecorino. Mix well and set aside to let the artichokes absorb the beaten egg mixture. Beat the 2 remaining eggs separately, mix with the rest of the grated pecorino and season with salt and pepper. In a round ovenproof dish, preferably earthenware, sauté 1 tablespoon of chopped parsley in a little oil. Then add the artichokes and beaten eggs. Bake at 200 °C until the mixture has a crusty golden topping. Serve at once.

Zucchine ripiene
(Stuffed courgettes)

Ingredients

8 medium-sized zucchine
250 g boiled meat
70 g soft bread
1 tablespoon of butter
1 glass of milk
2 eggs
30 g grated parmesan
nutmeg

Clean and wash the courgettes, cut into halves, scoop out the flesh and reserve. Blanch the courgette halves in boiling water, drain and lay out on a clean cloth to dry. Meanwhile, put the bread in a basin with a little milk and leave to soften. Chop the boiled beef, add the eggs, grated parmesan, salt, pepper, a pinch of nutmeg, the reserved courgette flesh and mix well. Then pass the mixture through a food mill and stuff the scooped-out courgettes with it. Place them in a pan greased with butter and bake in the oven at 170-180 °C for about 30 minutes. When the courgettes have turned golden brown, serve them hot.

Sweets

Buccellato
(Lemon bread)

Ingredients
400 g flour
150 g sugar
50 g butter
10 g brewer's yeast
2 eggs
1 organic lemon
2 tablespoons of milk
1 pinch of baking soda
1 pinch of salt

Sift the flour into a small heap, add the sugar, grated lemon rind, a salt and baking soda. Then add the eggs, the butter, that has been softened at room temperature and cut into pieces, and the brewer's yeast, dissolved in a little milk. Knead the dough with your hands until it is smooth and compact, then cover with a clean cloth and allow to stand for a about 2 hours. After this time, knead it again before placing in a buttered and floured 18-20 cm pie dish.

Bake in the oven at 180 °C for 40 minutes. Serve the buccellato cold, accompanied by cream or home-made jam, or by a glass of fine vinsanto to dip the slices in.

Recommended wine
Vinsanto Val d'Arbia

Budinone di riso
(Rice cake)

Ingredients
250 g pudding rice
125 g sugar
75 g mixed candied fruit
30 g butter
30 g pine nuts
30 g walnut kernels
1/2 l milk, 2 eggs
1/2 sachet vanilla essence
1/2 organic lemon
1/2 organic orange
powdered sugar
powdered chocolate

Pour the milk into a pan, bring to the boil, add the rice and sugar, cover and simmer for 35 minutes. If the rice shows a tendency to dry out too much, add a little warm water or milk. When done, remove from heat and allow to cool, stirring from time to time.

Meanwhile whip the eggs together with the vanilla, and add the candied fruit, melted butter, grated orange and lemon peel, the pine nuts and crushed walnuts. Fold the mixture into the rice, mixing thoroughly so that all the ingredients are carefully stirred in. Grease an 18-20 cm pudding dish, pour the mixture in, smooth its surface carefully, dust with the powdered sugar and powdered chocolate, then place in a hot oven at 220 °C. Bake for about 30 minutes, making sure that it does not brown too much. If necessary, cover with a sheet of aluminum foil. Test it for with a toothpick to see if it is done. When the toothpick comes out clean, the cake is cooked. Remove from the oven, let cool and turn out onto a rack.

Recommended wine
Vinsanto Carmignano

Castagnaccio
(Chestnut cake)

Ingredients
300 g chestnut flour
50 g pine nuts
50 g raisins
1 sprig rosemary
1/4 glass e.v. olive oil + oil
 for the pan
pinch of salt

"Castagnaccio" is one of the most typical and time-honoured cakes. It is best when served warm. Mix the chestnut flour in a bowl with a little water, whipping it to form a creamy without lumps. Add the oil, a pinch of salt, some pine nuts and some of the raisins, pre-soaked in warm water and squeezed out carefully. Mix thoroughly so that the nuts and raisins are evenly distributed throughout the batter, which should be very fluid. Grease with olive oil a rectangular baking pan, large enough so that the batter will fill it to a height of about 2 cm. Pour the batter in and sprinkle on it the remaining raisins and pine nuts; add a few rosemary needles. Bake in the oven at 200 °C for about 40 minutes. The chestnut cake is done when the top is cracked but not burned. Serve warm cut in squares.

Recommended wine
Vinsanto Bianco
Pisano di San Torpè

Cantuccini di Prato
(Almond biscuits)

Ingredients

300 g flour
200 g sugar
100 g shelled and peeled sweet almonds
3 eggs
1/2 organic orange
1 tablespoon anise seed
1/2 glass of milk
pinch of baking soda
pinch of salt
1 tablespoon butter

Recommended wine

Vinsanto Bianco Pisano di San Torpè

Sift the flour into a heap on the pastry board together with the baking soda.

Slowly add the sugar, pinch of salt, 1 teaspoon of grated orange peel, after removing the pith, the anise seed and almonds.

Break 2 eggs into these ingredients and work together carefully, adding a drop of milk if the dough is too stiff.

Then shape into 3 elongated rolls about 5 cm thick; place them on the oven tray greased with butter and brush them with the beaten yolk of the remaining egg.

Bake in the oven at 190 °C for 15 minutes.

Remove from the oven and cut up into slanting slices, to obtain the classic wedge shape of cantuccini. Put back in the oven for another 5 minutes.

Vinsanto

Vinsanto is a heavy wine that is produced by special techniques, mainly in Tuscany, from Trebbiano and Malvasia grapes, and in Trentino, where Nosiola and Pinot Bianco grapes are used.

The production technique calls for the use of naturally dried grapes and a long ageing process (from 3 to 5 years).

It is aged in small wooden barrels in special rooms where the evolutionary process of wine is controlled in an entirely different way from the usual, conferring on it a particularly pleasant taste. A meditation wine, generally served with desserts and sweets, it should be served cold.

Cavallucci
(Walnut biscuits)

Ingredients
500 g flour
300 g sugar
100 g powdered almonds
100 g candied orange peel
50 g liquid honey
30 g powdered anise seed
15 g mixed cinnamon,
10 g nutmeg and coriander
6 g creme of tartar
4 g baking soda
1 tablespoon butter

In a pan, preferably copper, melt over low heat 250 g of sugar with the honey until it reaches the 'fine thread' stage, then remove from heat and add the chopped walnut kernels, the powdered almonds, the finely chopped candied orange peel, powdered anise and spices. Mix the ingredients to form a smooth paste. Sift the flower into a heap on the pastry board, add the paste prepared as described above, add the baking soda and creme of tartar. Work the ingredients together with little water, kneading with your hands to form dough that is cohesive but soft. Shape the dough into small balls of about 30-40 g each, arrange in a buttered and floured oven tray, sprinkle with the remaining sugar and bake in the oven at 150 °C for 1 hour. Remove from the oven before the biscuits have become too dark, and allow to dry out before serving.

Recommended wine
Vinsanto
Montescudaio

Cenci
(Rag-shaped fritters)

Ingredients
400 g flour
250 g sugar
30 g anise seed
4 eggs
powdered vanilla essence
ammonium carbonate
1 organic orange
1 glass of vinsanto
pinch of salt
sunflower oil or lard
DUSTING:
vanilla-flavoured powdered
sugar

Traditionally associated with the carnival festivities, cenci can be served either hot or cold. The quantities recommended here are sufficient for about 8 people.

Wash the anise seeds and boil with the vinsanto for 1 minute, then set aside to cool, covered with a clean cloth; drain, reserving the vinsanto. Sift the flour into a heap on the pastry board, add the eggs, the reserved vinsanto, the sugar, and a pinch of salt. Work all these ingredients together, adding the flour a little at a time to form a smooth paste. Then add a pinch of ammonium carbonate and vanilla essence, and grated orange peel (without the pith), and knead well.

Roll out into a thin sheet of pastry with the rolling pin, dust with a little more flour, cut into lozenge shapes using a knife or a pastry cutter, and deep-fry immediately in hot oil or fat.

When they are golden brown, remove from the oil and drain, placing the cenci on paper towels. Lastly, sprinkle with vanilla-flavoured powdered sugar.

Recommended wine
Vinsanto Bianco
Pisano di San Torpè

Ciambelle di Pasqua
(Easter doughnuts)

The doses recommended here are ideal for preparing roughly 5 doughnuts.

The day before baking, prepare the basic mixture. Whip the sugar and egg yolks together in a bowl to form a frothy cream. Add the liqueur and the vanilla essence, then fold in the stiffly beaten egg whites, blending the ingredients delicately. Gently stir in the potato flour. Cover and leave in a cool place overnight.

The next day, sift the flour into a heap on the pastry board, add the previously prepared mixture, the melted and slightly cooled butter, the grated orange and lemon peel (without the pith) and the squeezed citrus juice. Add a pinch of salt and begin to work all the ingredients together, adding the flour to the liquid mixture a very little at a time.

As soon as the mixture begins to stiffen, add the

Ingredients
1 kg flour
500 g sugar
250 g butter
200 g potato flour
10 eggs
2 sachets of powdered vanilla essence
2 sachets of powdered vanilla-flavoured yeast
1 glass of mixed rosolio, maraschino and rum
2 organic oranges
1 organic lemon
granulated sugar
pinch of salt
1 tablespoon butter

yeast and knead with your hands to form a smooth dough. Divide it into the doughnut shapes, as follows: take a small ball of pastry, make a hole in the middle with your finger, and then hollow it out manually by swinging it round and round your finger to form a typical doughnut shape.

Place the doughnuts in buttered and floured oven pans, dredge with granulated sugar and bake immediately in a preheated oven at 200 °C for about 35 minutes. Do not open the oven during the first 15 minutes of baking, to keep the doughnuts from falling.

When they are golden brown and nicely puffed up, remove from the oven and place on a clean cloth to cool before serving.

Recommended wine
Vinsanto Carmignano

Cotognata
(Quince jelly)

Ingredients
5 kg quinces
1 kg Rennet apples
oranges and lemons
totalling 1 kg
1 stick vanilla
1 glass of brandy
(or bourbon)
sugar as needed

Cotognata is a kind of jelly made of quinces. Quince trees produce a highly fragrant fruit, sharp-tasting and with an elevated pectin content, making it ideal for jelly, as pectin is a natural gelatinizing substance.

Wash and cut the apples and quinces into pieces, place in a pot, preferably earthenware, and cook over moderate heat.

When they begin to ooze juice, add the peeled and sliced oranges and lemons. Cook over moderate heat for about 2 hours.

Then pass the fruit through a sieve, weigh the resulting pulp and add the same amount of sugar as the

114

weight of the pulp. Return the fruit to heat, adding the vanilla and the brandy (or bourbon), and boil for 1 hour. Remove from heat and, while still hot, pour in moulds lined with greased paper.

Fill each mould to the height of about 2 cm, then cover with aluminum foil. Leave the moulds in a cool place for about 10 days.

The jam is then ready to use.

Crogetti
(Citrus fritters)

Ingredients

1 kg flour
400 g sugar
200 g butter
10 eggs
2 organic lemons
2 organic oranges
1 small glass of rum
1 small glass of rosolio
2 sachets vanilla-flavoured baking powder
1 pinch salt
vanilla-flavoured powdered sugar
sunflower oil (or e.v. olive oil)

Crogetti are the typical fritters of the Carnival period in southern Tuscany.

The quantities given here are suitable for almost 10/15 people, as crogetti are never prepared in small quantities.

Sift the flour into a heap on the kitchen counter, add the eggs, melted butter, sugar, a small pinch of salt, the grated lemon and orange rind (without the pith) and the liqueur.

Delicately knead the pastry. As soon as it begins to stick together, add the vanilla-flavoured baking powder. Continue to knead until a smooth paste is obtained, then roll the dough with the rolling pin into a sheet of pastry that is not too thin.

Cut it into lozenges and fry in boiling oil.

As soon as they turn golden brown, drain and let dry on paper towels. Serve with a dusting of powdered sugar.

Recommended wine
Vinsanto Pomino

Fragolata
(Strawberry bowl)

Ingredients
500 g strawberries
200 g vanilla-flavoured powdered sugar
50 g bitter chocolate
1/2 l cream
1/2 lemon
1/2 orange
1 small glass of cognac
1 teaspoon of curaçao
DECORATION:
a few slices of organic orange

Book Festival 2011.
Great / Easy!
Maint Ame

Whip the cream with 150 g of vanilla-flavoured powdered sugar and heap into a dome-shaped mould after incorporating the chopped chocolate. Place the mould in the freezer for at least 3 hours. Meanwhile, clean and rinse the strawberries and cut into pieces; place in a bowl with the lemon juice for 1 hour. Drain the strawberries well, place them in a bowl and add the cognac, the orange juice and remaining vanilla-flavoured powdered sugar; leave for 2 hours.

Then remove the mould from the freezer, plunge for a few seconds into warm water and turn out onto a tray. Pour the drained strawberries onto the mound of frozen cream, garnish with a few slices of orange, sprinkle with a little curaçao and serve.

Frittelle di San Giuseppe
(Saint Joseph's fritters)

Ingredients
300 g pudding rice
100 g sugar
100 g flour
1 l milk
3 eggs
1 organic lemon
1 organic orange
pinch of salt
sunflower oil (or e.v. olive oil)
vanilla-flavoured powdered sugar

Heat 1/2 litre of milk in a pan, and keep the remaining 1/2 litre warm in a separate pan. Bring the contents of the first pan to the boil, then pour the rice in together with a pinch of salt. Simmer, stirring frequently and adding a little more milk periodically, until the rice is well cooked and soft.

Remove from heat and allow the rice to cool, then add the beaten eggs, flour, grated lemon and orange peel (without the pith), and mix the ingredients together very thoroughly. Heat up a generous quantity of oil in a frying pan and when it is smoking hot but not boiling or burning, spoon in the mixture in level tablespoons.

Fry the fritters on both sides, then drain on paper towels. When they have cooled slightly, sprinkle them with vanilla-flavoured powdered sugar. If preferred, the rice can be prepared the day before and left to stand all night in a covered basin.

Recommended wine
Vinsanto Carmignano

Pan co' santi
(Walnut and raisin loaf)

Ingredients

2 kg flour, type 0
200 g walnut kernels
200 g raisins
200 g sugar
50 g brewer's yeast
50 g shelled and peeled hazelnuts or almonds
15 g powdered black pepper
10 g salt
2 tablespoons lard
1 tablespoon anise seed
1 organic lemon
1 egg
1 heaping tablespoon butter
e.v. olive oil

The quantities given here are for cake large enough for about 10 people.

Chop the hazelnuts, grate the lemon rind, wash the anise seed; wash the raisins and soak them in a little water. Reserve a few walnuts and chop the rest, then sauté in a pan with the lard.

Allow to cool, then add the well squeezed raisins, reserving a few for later use. Dissolve the yeast with a few drops of warm water. Sift the flour into a small heap on the pastry board, add the dissolved yeast, the sautéed walnuts and raisins, and begin to work the ingredients together, gradually adding a few drops of warm water.

When the dough begins to stick together, add the sugar, salt, pepper, almonds or hazelnuts, lemon rind (without the pith), and anise seed.

Continue to knead the dough thoroughly, then set aside to rise in a wicker basket covered with a clean floured cloth. Wrap the entire basket in a blanket and leave in a warm place, away from drafts, for at least 3 hours. Then divide the dough into balls of about 500 g each, flour them, brush them with beaten egg white and let rest for a further 30 minutes.

Then place the loaves in an oven dish, decorate with a few raisins and some walnut kernels and bake in a preheated oven at 210 °C for about 35 minutes. Switch off the oven, open the oven door and leave open for 5 minutes, to dry the loaves completely.

Remove from oven. Pan co' santi is best if left to rest for at least 24 hours before eating.

Recommended wine
Vinsanto Carmignano

Pasta pesata
(Weighed dough)

Ingredients
500 g of whole eggs with the shells removed
500 g sugar
500 g flour
30 g butter
1 sachet vanilla-flavoured baking powder
1 organic lemon

For this recipe, the shelled eggs must be weighed. After grating the lemon rind, whip the eggs with the sugar, and when they are creamy and frothy, add the sifted flour, folding it in delicately from the bottom upwards with a wooden spoon. Then add the grated lemon rind (without the pitch) and the yeast.

Generously butter a 20 cm pie-dish, pour in the mixture and place immediately in an oven preheated to around 170 °C. During the baking time, do not open the oven door for any reason. When done, wait another 30 minutes before removing the cake, which will be thoroughly dry, golden and puffed up. Let it cool before slicing and serving.

Pasta pesata, or weighed dough, can also be used as a base for other sweets and cakes, cream desserts or biscuits.

Recommended wine
Vinsanto Bianco
Pisano di San Torpè

118

Pasterelle senesi
(Sienese pastries)

Ingredients
300 g flour
300 g walnut kernels
300 g sugar
50 g candied orange peel
2 tablespoons anise seed
1 pinch powdered cinnamon
1 tablespoon butter

Mix and cream the sugar in 1/2 glass of water to form a syrup. Sift the flour into a heap on the pastry board, add the finely chopped walnuts and the sugar syrup, the crushed anise seed, cinnamon and finely chopped candied orange rind.

Work the ingredients together to form a stiff paste, then shape into balls each roughly the size of a walnut. Roll them out into oval-shaped pastries and press them to a thickness of 1/2 cm.

Butter the oven tray, place the pastries on the tray and bake in a preheated oven at a temperature not over 150 °C for about 35-40 minutes, without letting them brown. When they are done, turn the oven off and leave them in the warm oven for a few minutes. Then remove each pastry carefully from the tray and let cool before eating.

These pastries will keep for a long time when stored in a hermetically sealed container.

Recommended wine
Vinsanto
Montescudaio

Neccio
(Chestnut crêpe)

Ingredients
500 g chestnut flour
200 g fresh ricotta
7 walnuts
1 organic orange
1 sprig rosemary
pinch of salt
e.v. olive oil

Wash and finely chop the rosemary and orange peel; break the walnut kernels into small pieces. Sift the chestnut flour into a bowl together with a pinch of salt, and then slowly add as much warm water as is needed to form a fairly thin and runny batter. Stir constantly to avoid lumps. Add the rosemary, orange peel and walnut kernels. Mix well, then pour the batter into a greased oven dish.

Dribble a little oil on top and bake at 190 °C for about 30 minutes, then serve hot with the ricotta spread thickly on top.

Recommended wine
Vinsanto Pomino

Pasticcini fiorentini
(Florentines)

Ingredients
150 g butter
150 g sugar
150 g shelled and peeled almonds
7 tablespoons cream
2-3 tablespoons liquid honey
1 tablespoon butter
GARNISH:
1 bar of semi-sweet chocolate
cherries in syrup

Chop half of the almonds and cut the remaining half into wafer-thin slices. Put the butter, cream, honey and sugar together in a pan, place over moderate heat and cook for about 10 minutes, stirring with a wooden spoon until the sugar begins to caramelise.

Add the almonds to the mixture and mix well. Scoop small heaps of the mixture onto a well greased oven tray, using a spoon dipped into cold water before each scoop. Take care not to place the little heaps too close to one another, as these delicate almond biscuits may run into each other and crumble. When they are arranged on the tray, flatten each one a little on top with the spoon. Bake at about 180 °C, placing the tray on the highest rack in the oven, for 15-20 minutes. Remove the tray from the oven and detach the biscuits carefully.

Meanwhile, cut the cherries into small pieces and dissolve the chocolate over simmering water. When the chocolate has melted, combine it with the chopped cherries. Spread a thick layer of this chocolate mixture on the lower side of the cookies, and set to dry on a rack upside down.

Recommended wine
Vinsanto Pomino

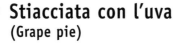

Stiacciata con l'uva
(Grape pie)

Ingredients
300 g risen bread dough
150 g sugar
1 bunch black grapes
1 tablespoon lard
1 tablespoon butter
powdered sugar

Knead the dough on a pastry board, add the lard and 2 tablespoons sugar, then let stand for an hour, covered with a cloth. Wash the grapes well, then peel and remove pips from each individual grape; reserve some of the grapes and crush the others coarsely with a fork. Knead the dough again a little, then divide it into 2 halves and roll it with a rolling-pin into 2 thick discs. Use one to line the inside of a 20 cm pie pan greased with butter, then place the crushed grapes on the pastry. Dust with the sugar, then cover with the other pastry disc, pinching the edges together.

Decorate with the remaining whole grapes and bake at 200 °C for 30 minutes. When ready to serve, sprinkle the grape pie with powdered sugar.

Recommended wine
Vinsanto Carmignano

Torta mandorlata
(Almond tart)

Ingredients
400 g plain flour
300 g butter
200 g sugar
150 g mixed nuts composed of walnuts, almonds and hazelnuts
1 lemon
1 orange
2 eggs
1 small spoonful of powdered yeast
apple jelly
bitter chocolate
pinch of salt

Gently roast the nuts, then sift the flour into a small heap on a pastry board, add the melted butter, sugar, egg yolks, pinch of salt, grated lemon and orange peel, a small amount of roasted nuts, and work the ingredients together carefully but gently, finally adding the yeast. The aim is to obtain a smooth paste without pummelling the dough too much. Roll the pastry out to medium thickness, then cut out a disc, place in a pie-dish and cover with roasted nuts and a generous amount of jam. Cut out a second pastry disk and use to cover the first;

baste the surface with egg white and sprinkle with the remaining nuts and chopped chocolate.

Bake in a moderate oven and check periodically to make sure it is drying out well; remove when it has taken a golden brown color, allow to cool and turn out on a rack.

Recommended wine
Vin Santo Pomino

Serve sliced, accompanied by whipped cream if you wish.

Ricciarelli di Siena
(Almond curls)

Ingredients

250 g powdered sugar
150 g shelled and peeled sweet almonds
15 g shelled and peeled bitter almonds
1 egg
20 confectionery wafers

Powder the almonds with a meat hammer or a food grinder. Add most of the powdered sugar and mix well, then whip the egg white until stiff, and delicately fold it into the almond paste, one tablespoon at a time. When the paste becomes too stiff to be mixed with a spoon, work it with your hands on the kitchen pastry board dusted with a little powdered sugar.

Knead until the paste is smooth, then roll out with the rolling pin to a thickness of about 1-1.5 cm, and cut into discs the size of the confectionery wafers. Place the confectionery wafers on an oven tray and then place an almond paste disc on each wafer. Cover with a teacloth and let rest for 1 hour in a cool place. Bake in a preheated oven at 160 °C for about 30 minutes, without letting the biscuits brown.

Remove from the oven, allow to cool and serve with a sprinkling of powdered sugar after having trimmed **Recommended wine** off any excess wafer protruding from the almond *Vinsanto Carmignano* discs.

INDEX OF RECIPES

Eggs

Fish

Meat

Side dishes

Sweets

Basic recipes

More about...